500 Recipes

Recipes

Cook's Bible

igloobooks

Published in 2014
by Igloo Books Ltd
Cottage Farm
Sywell
NN6 0BJ
www.igloobooks.com

Copyright© 2013 Igloo Books Ltd

SHE001 1213
2 4 6 8 10 9 7 5 3
ISBN 978-1-78197-900-6

Food photography and recipe development: PhotoCuisine UK
Front and back cover images © PhotoCuisine UK

Printed and manufactured in China

500 Recipes
Cook's Bible

igloobooks

CONTENTS

EGGS

Pancakes with Chocolate Sauce

1

MAKES 16

PREPARATION TIME 25 MINUTES

COOKING TIME 20 MINUTES

INGREDIENTS

225g / 8 oz / 1 cup plain (all purpose) flour
2 tsp baking powder
1 tsp caster (superfine) sugar
Pinch salt
300ml / 10 fl oz / 1 ¼ cups milk
2 eggs
1 tsp vanilla extract
Vegetable oil
Mixed berries such as blueberries, raspberries and strawberries

FOR THE CHOCOLATE SAUCE
1 jar Nutella (200g)
100ml / 3 ½ fl oz / ½ cup double cream

- Mix together the flour, baking powder, sugar and salt in a bowl.
- Whisk together the milk, eggs and vanilla extract.
- Mix the wet ingredients into the dry ingredients to a thick smooth batter then leave to rest for 15 minutes.
- Heat a thin film of vegetable oil in the pan and add large dollops of batter to the pan to make circles around 5cm across. Cook until they bubble on top, then turn over and cook for another 1-2 minutes.
- Remove from the pan and keep warm while you make the rest.
- Heat the Nutella with the cream in a small pan to make the chocolate sauce, then serve with the pancakes and berries.

Pancakes with Chocolate Cointreau Sauce

2

- Add 2 tbsp of Cointreau or orange liqueur to the Nutella and cream while heating.

3

Toasted Muffin with Scrambled Egg

SERVES 4

PREPARATION TIME 5 MINUTES

COOKING TIME 8 MINUTES

INGREDIENTS

4 English muffins, split horizontally
6 eggs
40g / 1 oz / ¼ cup butter
6 tsp double cream
Salt and pepper

- Crack the eggs into a bowl and beat lightly.
- Heat most of the butter in a pan until foaming, then stir in the eggs.
- Cook gently, stirring thoroughly with a wooden spoon moving the eggs around the pan until lightly cooked with some liquid egg still left.
- Stir in the cream and season.
- Serve immediately with the toasted muffins.

Toasted Muffin with Herby Scrambled Eggs

4

- Stir in ½ bunch chopped chives or chervil with the cream.

5

SERVES 4

Ham, Tomato & Chive Omelette

- Heat the oil in a large frying pan and cook the tomatoes for a few seconds.
- Season the eggs, then pour into the pan. Swirl the pan to move the eggs into all the corners and coat everything.
- Top with the ham and sprinkle over the chives.
- Place under a hot grill for about 5-6 minutes to set the frittata – keep checking it to ensure nothing burns.
- Allow to cool a little then cut into wedges and serve.

PREPARATION TIME 5 MINUTES

COOKING TIME 8 MINUTES

INGREDIENTS

1 tbsp olive oil
3 slices prosciutto, torn into strips
6 eggs, lightly beaten
Salt and pepper
8 cherry tomatoes, halved
1 bunch chives, chopped

Ham Mushroom Chive Omelette

6

- Cook 8 quartered button mushrooms for 5 minutes as a substitution for the tomatoes.

7

SERVES 4

Scotch Eggs

- Place 4 eggs in a pan of simmering water. Cook for 1 minute, then cover with a lid, remove from the heat and leave for 5 minutes exactly.
- When the time is up, remove from the heat and chill.
- Mix together the meat, herbs, salt and pepper, mustard and mix well. Divide into quarters.
- Peel the boiled eggs. Place the beaten eggs, flour and breadcrumbs in dishes in a line.
- Lay a piece of clingfilm on the work surface and cover with a quarter of the forcemeat. Lay another piece on top and squish until large enough to coat the boiled egg.
- Roll an egg in the flour then place in the centre of the forcemeat. Encase the egg in the meat. Dip each egg into the flour, then beaten egg then breadcrumbs. Repeat for all 4.
- Heat the oil and cook the eggs 2 at a time for 6-7 minutes until crisp and golden.

PREPARATION TIME 25 MINUTES

COOKING TIME 6-7 MINUTES

INGREDIENTS

4 eggs + 2 eggs beaten
200g / 7 oz / ¾ cup sausagemeat
200g / 7 oz / ¾ cup minced pork
1 tbsp parsley, finely chopped
½ tbsp sage, finely chopped
½ tsp ground mace
1 tbsp grain or Dijon mustard (optional)
2 tbsp plain (all purpose) flour
100g / 3 ½ oz / ½ cup fine breadcrumbs, seasoned with a pinch of Cayenne
Vegetable oil

Black Pudding Scotch Eggs

8

- Substitute the minced pork for an equal amount of crumbled black pudding for an earthier treat.

Cherry Tomato, Coriander & Feta Tortilla

9

SERVES 4

PREPARATION TIME 30 MINUTES

COOKING TIME 30 MINUTES

INGREDIENTS

6 eggs
1 tbsp crème fraîche
8 cherry tomatoes, halved
100g feta cheese, cubed
6 sprigs coriander (cilantro),
chopped
Olive oil
Salt and pepper

- Preheat the oven to 180°C (160° fan) / 350F / gas 5.
- Beat the eggs with the creme fraîche in a large bowl.
- Add tomatoes, feta, coriander and season then mix together carefully.
- Oil a large frying pan, then pour the mixture in and bake for about 35 minutes until puffed and golden. The egg should be cooked through.
- Cut into squares and serve warm or cold.

Cherry Tomato, Parsley & Goats Cheese Tortilla

10

- Try goats cheese instead of feta and substitute the parsley for coriander.

Eggs Benedict

11

SERVES 4

PREPARATION TIME 10 MINUTES

COOKING TIME 3-5 MINUTES

INGREDIENTS

4 eggs
4 thick slices ham
4 English muffins
30g / 1 oz butter

FOR THE HOLLANDAISE SAUCE
175g / 6 oz / ¾ cup butter
1 tbsp white wine vinegar
2 tbsp lemon juice
3 egg yolks
Pinch salt

- Melt the butter in a pan. Place the vinegar and lemon juice in another pan and boil.
- Place the egg yolks and salt in a food processor and whiz briefly, then with it still running, very gradually add the hot lemon juice and vinegar.
- Again very very slowly add the melted butter until the sauce emulsifies. Keep warm in a bowl over hot water while you cook the eggs.
- Poach the eggs in boiling water for about 3 minutes for a runny yolk. Remove to kitchen paper and leave to drain.
- Cut the muffins in half horizontally and lightly toast the cut sides, then butter.
- Place the muffins on a plate and lay over the slices of ham.
- Top with the poached eggs and hollandaise sauce.

Eggs Benedict with Watercress

12

- Wilt a small bag of chopped watercress in a little butter then serve under the poached egg for a peppery hit.

Eggs Florentine with Mornay Sauce

13

SERVES 4

Eggs Florentine with Tomato Sauce   14

- Instead of making a mornay sauce, simply simmer a can of chopped tomatoes until reduced, season well and pour over.

Eggs Florentine with Bacon   15

- Add 2 rashers of chopped streaky bacon to the pan before you wilt the spinach.

Eggs Florentine with Baked Mushrooms   16

- For low-carb addicts, serve the poached egg and spinach on top of a buttery oven-baked field mushroom.

PREPARATION TIME 5 MINUTES

COOKING TIME 8 MINUTES

INGREDIENTS

2 handfuls spinach leaves
1 tbsp butter
4 eggs
4 slices bread, toasted

FOR THE MORNAY SAUCE
150ml / 5 fl oz / ⅔ cup milk
150ml / 5 fl oz / ⅔ cup single cream
1 tsp Dijon mustard
1 tbsp plain (all purpose) flour
1 ½ tbsp butter
50g / 1 ¾ oz / ¼ cup Cheddar, grated
1 tbsp Parmesan, grated
½ bunch parsley, chopped
Squeeze of lemon juice
Salt and pepper

- To make the Mornay sauce, whisk the milk, cream, mustard, flour and butter in a pan over medium heat until smooth and thick.
- Whisk in the cheeses and stir to melt, then cook the sauce over a low heat for 5 minutes or so to cook out the flour.
- Add the parsley, season well, set aside and keep warm.
- Poach the eggs in boiling water for about 3 minutes for a runny yolk. Remove to kitchen paper and leave to drain.
- Wilt the spinach in a pan, then squeeze out any excess moisture and stir in the butter to melt.
- Toast the bread and top with the spinach. Place an egg on top, then spoon over the Mornay sauce.

17

SERVES 4

Stuffed Tomatoes

PREPARATION TIME 10 MINUTES

COOKING TIME 10-15 MINUTES

....

INGREDIENTS

6 eggs, lightly beaten
40g / 1 oz / ¼ cup butter
6 tsp double cream
Salt and pepper
1 tbsp parsley, chopped
4 large tomatoes

- Preheat the oven to 200°C (180° fan) / 400F / gas 7.
- Heat most of the butter in a pan until foaming, then stir in the eggs.
- Cook gently, stirring thoroughly with a wooden spoon moving the eggs around the pan until lightly cooked with some liquid egg still left.
- Stir in the cream and parsley and season.
- Core the tomatoes and scoop a little of the flesh from inside, then spoon the egg into the cavity.
- Place in a roasting and cook for 10-15 minutes or until the tomatoes have softened.

Mushroom Stuffed Baked Tomatoes   18

- Add 6 button mushrooms, finely chopped to the pan before the eggs.

19

SERVES 4

Vanilla Baked Egg Custard

PREPARATION TIME 10 MINUTES

COOKING TIME 50-60 MINUTES

....

INGREDIENTS

500ml / 1 pint / 2 cups milk
1 tsp vanilla extract
40g / 1 ½ oz caster (superfine) sugar
3 eggs, lightly beaten
Grated nutmeg

- Preheat the oven to 180°C (160° fan) / 350F / gas 5.
- Heat the milk and vanilla in a pan until nearly at boiling point then set aside to cool for a minute.
- Meanwhile whisk the sugar with the eggs.
- Pour the scented milk over the eggs, whisking continually until thickened and smooth.
- Strain into a buttered ovenproof 1 pint baking dish. Bake for 50-60 minutes until just set.
- Serve with freshly grated nutmeg over the top.

Rose Egg Custard   20

- Add 2 drops of rosewater to the custard mixture for a scented version of this classic.

21

SERVES 6 # Courgette, Tomato and Feta Frittata

- Preheat the oven to 180°C (160° fan) / 350F / gas 5.
- Beat the eggs with the crème fraîche in a large bowl.
- Add the courgettes, tomatoes, feta, thyme leaves and season then mix together carefully.
- Oil a large frying pan, then pour the mixture in and bake for about 35 minutes until puffed and golden. The egg should be cooked through.
- Cut into squares and serve warm or cold.

PREPARATION TIME 30 MINUTES

COOKING TIME 35 MINUTES

INGREDIENTS

8 eggs
1 tbsp crème fraîche
2 courgettes (zucchini), finely diced
Handful sun dried tomatoes, finely chopped
100g feta cheese, cubed
6 sprigs thyme
Olive oil
Salt and pepper

Courgette, Tomato and Taleggio Frittata

22

- Substitute melting Taleggio cheese for the cubed feta for an oozing frittata.

23

SERVES 6 # Green Asparagus Frittata

- Preheat the oven to 180°C (160° fan) / 350F / gas 5.
- Beat the eggs with the crème fraîche in a large bowl.
- Snap the woody ends off the asparagus and discard. Cut the asparagus into short lengths.
- Fry the onion gently in 2 tbsp olive oil until deep gold and soft – about 20 minutes
- Pour the egg mixture in, add the asparagus and distribute evenly.
- Bake for about 35 minutes until puffed and golden. The egg should be cooked through.
- Cut into squares and serve warm or cold

PREPARATION TIME 30 MINUTES

COOKING TIME 35 MINUTES

INGREDIENTS

8 eggs
1 tbsp crème fraîche
1 bunch asparagus
1 onion, peeled and thickly sliced
Olive oil
Salt and pepper

Asparagus and Ham Frittata

24

- Add 2 chopped slices of ham just before baking to set off the sweet flavour of the asparagus.

Spanish Style Scrambled Eggs

25

SERVES 4

PREPARATION TIME 5 MINUTES

COOKING TIME 15 MINUTES

....

INGREDIENTS

1 tbsp groundnut oil
1 red pepper, deseeded and finely
sliced
6 eggs
40g / 1 oz / ¼ cup butter
6 tsp double cream
Salt and pepper
1 tbsp chives, chopped
4 slices Serrano or prosciutto ham,
torn into strips
4 thick slices bread, toasted and
buttered

- Heat the oil in a pan and cook the peppers until softened and sweet.
- Crack the eggs into a bowl and beat lightly.
- Add the butter to the pan, then stir in the eggs.
- Cook gently, stirring thoroughly with a wooden spoon moving the eggs around the pan until lightly cooked with some liquid egg still left.
- Stir in the cream and chives and ham and season.
- Serve immediately on toast.

Spanish-Style Cheesy Eggs   26
- Add 2 tbsp finely shaved Manchego cheese on top just before serving.

Scrambled Eggs & Mushrooms on Toast

27

SERVES 4

PREPARATION TIME 5 MINUTES

COOKING TIME 10 MINUTES

....

INGREDIENTS

40g / 1 oz / ¼ cup butter
80g / 2 ½ oz / ⅓ cup button
mushrooms, halved
6 eggs
6 tsp double cream
Salt and pepper
1 tbsp parsley, chopped
4 thick slices bread, toasted and
buttered

- Heat the butter in a pan and cook the mushrooms until golden and all the excess moisture has evaporated.
- Crack the eggs into a bowl and beat lightly.
- Stir the eggs into the pan and cook gently, stirring thoroughly with a wooden spoon moving the eggs around the pan until lightly cooked with some liquid egg still left.
- Stir in the cream and parsley and season.
- Serve immediately with the toast.

Scrambled Eggs and   28
Mushrooms with Bacon
- Fry a rasher of back bacon and place on the toast under the mushrooms for a more substantial meal.

29

SERVES 4

Baked Egg with Garlic & Tomato

Spicy Baked Eggs   30

- Add ½ finely chopped red chilli over the tomato before the egg for a real livener.

Baked Eggs with Cheese and Tomato   31

- Sprinkle a handful of cheese over the top of the eggs 5 minuts before the end.

Baked Eggs on Toasted Bread   32

- Five minutes before the end, gently toast 4 slices of bread and spread with a little butter. Slide the eggs on top and serve.

PREPARATION TIME 10 MINUTES

COOKING TIME 15-20 MINUTES

INGREDIENTS

60g / 2 oz / ¼ cup butter
2 tomatoes, halved
1 clove garlic, crushed
4 eggs
30g / 1 oz butter
Salt and pepper

- Preheat the oven to 190°C (170° fan) / 375F / gas 5.
- Butter 4 ramekin dishes generously and place a tomato half in the bottom topped with a little garlic and salt and pepper.
- Crack the eggs into the ramekins on top of the tomato and dot with butter.
- Place the ramekins in a roasting tin, pour in enough boiling water to come halfway up the sides of the ramekins and bake in the oven for 15-20 minutes or until the eggs are just set.

Tuna and Courgette Tortilla

33

SERVES 4

PREPARATION TIME 10 MINUTES

COOKING TIME 20 MINUTES

....

INGREDIENTS

4 tbsp olive oil
1 courgette (zucchini), quartered
and sliced
6 free-range eggs
200 g / 7 oz canned tuna, drained
and flaked
oregano, to garnish

- Heat half the oil in a non-stick frying pan and fry the courgettes for 5 minutes.
- Meanwhile, gently beat the eggs in a jug to break up the yolks. When the courgettes are ready, stir them into the eggs with the tuna and season with salt and pepper.
- Heat the rest of the oil in the frying pan then pour in the egg mixture.
- Cook over a gentle heat for 6 – 8 minutes or until the egg has set round the outside, but the centre is still a bit runny.
- Turn it out onto a plate, then slide it back into the pan and cook the other side for 4 – 6 minutes.
- Leave to cool for 5 minutes then cut into wedges and serve, garnished with oregano.

Salmon Courgette Tortilla 34

- Use canned salmon instead of tuna.

Mixed Pepper Tortilla

35

SERVES 6

PREPARATION TIME 30 MINUTES

COOKING TIME 35 MINUTES

....

INGREDIENTS

1 red pepper, deseeded and cut in
half
1 yellow pepper, deseeded and cut
in half
4 tbsp olive oil
1 clove garlic, crushed
8 eggs
1 tbsp crème fraîche
½ bunch parsley, chopped
Olive oil
Salt and pepper

- Preheat the oven to 200°C (180° fan) / 400F / gas 7.
- Place the pepper halves in a roasting in, drizzle with oil and roast for about 30 minutes or until soft and blackened.
- Remove from the tin, place in a freezer bag and leave to steam.
- Once cooled, remove the skins from the peppers and roughly chop the flesh.
- Beat the eggs with the crème fraîche in a large bowl.
- Add the peppers, garlic and parsley and season then mix together carefully.
- Oil a large frying pan, then pour the mixture in and bake at 180°C / 350F for about 35 minutes until puffed and golden. The egg should be cooked through.
- Cut into squares and serve warm or cold.

Mixed Pepper and Serrano Ham Tortilla 36

- Stir in slivers of Serrano ham before baking for a meaty twist.

37

SERVES 4 # French Toast

French Toast with Bacon & Maple Syrup

38

- Omit the vanilla extract and serve with fried or grilled rashers of streaky bacon or prosciutto and maple syrup.

Savoury French Toast

39

- Omit the vanilla extract and add some finely chopped chives to the egg/milk mixture.

Cheesy French Toast

40

- Omit the vanilla extract and add 50g/1 ¾ oz finely grated Parmesan to the egg/milk mixture.

PREPARATION TIME 15 MINUTES

COOKING TIME 10 MINUTES

....

INGREDIENTS

1 thick slice white bread per person (or more if you're hungry...)
2 eggs, beaten
300ml / 10 fl oz / 1 ¼ cups full fat milk or single cream
1 tsp vanilla extract
½ tsp ground cinnamon
2 tbsp vegetable oil

- Whisk together the eggs, milk, vanilla and cinnamon and pour into a bowl.
- Lay the bread into the mixture, soaking it thoroughly for a few minutes.
- Heat the oil in a pan and gently fry the bread triangles 2 at a time until golden and crisp on each side.
- Serve hot.

SAUCES AND STOCKS

41

MAKES 100ML Mustard Vinaigrette

- Whisk together the vinegar, mustard and salt until thick.
- Add the sugar, then whisk the olive oil in slowly to make a thick emulsion.
- Adjust the seasoning if necessary then serve with salad.

PREPARATION TIME 5 MINUTES

INGREDIENTS

1 tbsp red wine vinegar
1 tbsp Dijon mustard
Pinch salt
Pinch sugar
6 tbsp extra virgin olive oil
Black pepper

42

Pesto

MAKES 100ML

PREPARATION TIME 10 MINUTES

INGREDIENTS

2 handfuls pine nuts
1 clove garlic, peeled and chopped
2 bunches basil
80g / 3 oz / ⅓ cup Parmesan, grated
Extra virgin olive oil
Salt and pepper

- Add the pine nuts to a frying pan over medium heat and lightly toast for a few seconds until golden.
- Place in a food processor with the garlic, basil and Parmesan.
- Whiz the ingredients in a food processor until roughly blended, stirring in enough olive oil to loosen.
- Store in the refrigerator for up to 3 days.

43

Mint Mayonnaise

MAKES 275ML

PREPARATION TIME 10 MINUTES

INGREDIENTS

2 egg yolks
½ clove garlic, crushed
1 tsp mustard powder
1 tsp salt
Black pepper

130ml / 4 ½ fl oz / ½ cup groundnut oil
130ml / 4 ½ fl oz / ½ cup olive oil
White wine vinegar
½ bunch mint leaves, finely chopped

- Place the egg yolks in a bowl with the garlic, mustard powder, salt and pepper. Whisk well.
- Using an electric whisk or hand whisk, pour in the oils one drop at a time, whisking each one in thoroughly.
- Once the mixture begins to thicken, then add the oil a little faster, whisking well.
- After half the oil has been added, stir in 1 tsp of vinegar. Add the remaining oil in a thin trickle, constantly whisking. Season and add the mint.
- If the mixture curdles, put an egg yolk in a clean bowl, add the curdled mixture drop by drop whisking it in, then continue with the remaining oil.
- Store for up to 7 days in the refrigerator.

44

MAKES 100ML # Mustard & Mint Vinaigrette

PREPARATION TIME 5 MINUTES

INGREDIENTS

1 tbsp red wine vinegar
1 tbsp Dijon mustard
Pinch salt
Pinch sugar
6 tbsp extra virgin olive oil
Black pepper
½ bunch mint leaves, finely chopped

- Whisk together the vinegar, mustard and salt until thick.
- Add the sugar, then whisk the olive oil in slowly to make a thick emulsion.
- Whisk in the mint leaves.
- Adjust the seasoning if necessary then serve with salad.

Mustard Tarragon Vinaigrette   45

- Substitute tarragon for the mint leaves for a French twist.

46

SERVES 4-6 # Béarnaise Sauce

PREPARATION TIME 5 MINUTES

COOKING TIME 15 MINUTES

INGREDIENTS

1 tbsp tarragon, chopped
1 shallot, finely chopped
6 black peppercorns, crushed
2 tbsp white wine vinegar
150ml / 5 fl oz / ⅔ cup dry white wine
3 egg yolks
1 tsp mustard powder
25g / 1 oz butter at room temperature
180g / 6 oz / ¾ cup butter, melted
Salt

- Put the tarragon, shallot, peppercorns, vinegar and wine in a small pan and reduce by a third until there are about 3 tbsp liquid left. Strain.
- Whisk the egg yolks and mustard together in a bowl over a pan of barely simmering water.
- Whisk in the vinegar reduction, add a tbsp water and whisk.
- Beat in the 25g butter a little at a time, then slowly trickle in the melted butter a drop at a time, continually whisking, until the sauce has emulsified and thickened.
- Season and keep warm until needed.

Choron Sauce   47

- Whisk ½ tbsp tomato puree into the sauce at the end.

48

SERVES 4

Classic Hollandaise Sauce

- Place the vinegar, water, onion, mace, bay leaf and peppercorns in a small pan and reduce to about 1 tbsp. Strain into a bowl, add 1 tbsp water.
- Whisk the egg yolks into the reduction.
- Place the bowl over a pan of barely simmering water and add a little of the butter, whisking until it has melted.
- Add the butter a little at a time, whisking continually, until the mixture emulsifies and thickens.
- Cook very gently for 2 minutes, then add a little lemon juice and season.

PREPARATION TIME 5 MINUTES

COOKING TIME 10-15 MINUTES

INGREDIENTS

2 tbsp white wine vinegar
2 tbsp water
1 slice onion
Pinch ground mace
1 bay leaf
6 black peppercorns, left whole
3 egg yolks
180g / 6 oz / ¾ cup butter at room temperature
Squeeze of lemon juice
Salt and white pepper

Herb Hollandaise   49

- Stir in ¼ bunch finely chopped chervil, tarragon or parsley at the end of cooking.

50

MAKES 200ML

Tartare Sauce

- Finely chop the shallot and gherkins.
- Place all of the ingredients into a bowl, adding the mayonnaise last.
- Mix well to combine all of the ingredients.
- Adjust the seasoning to taste using salt and pepper and serve.

PREPARATION TIME 10 MINUTES

INGREDIENTS

200g / 7 oz / ¾ cup mayonnaise
1 shallot
2 gherkins (cornichons)
2 tbsp capers, drained
½ bunch parsley, chopped
½ lemon, juiced
Salt and pepper

Sauce Gribiche   51

- Stir in 1 finely chopped hard boiled egg.

52 SERVES 4 Cranberry Sauce

PREPARATION TIME 5 MINUTES

COOKING TIME 10-15 MINUTES

INGREDIENTS

500g / 1lb / 2 cups fresh cranberries
200g / 7 oz / ¾ cup sugar (you may need more)
Zest and juice of 1 orange
1 tbsp port or cassis

- Place the ingredients in a pan and add 4 tbsp water.
- Bring to a boil then reduce the heat and cook until the cranberries have burst and the sauce has thickened.
- Pour into a bowl and check if it needs more sugar – it will thicken further as it cools.

Cranberry Sauce with Mustard 53

- Stirring in 2 heaped tbsp grain mustard helps add depth and heat.

54 SERVES 4 Red Wine & Mushroom Sauce

PREPARATION TIME 5 MINUTES

COOKING TIME 30-40 MINUTES

INGREDIENTS

50g / 1 ¾ oz / ¼ cup dried mushrooms
500ml / 1 pint / 2 cups beef or chicken stock
25g / 1 oz butter
1 shallot, finely chopped
½ tbsp plain (all purpose) flour
100ml / 3 ½ fl oz / ½ cup red wine
1 bay leaf
1 sprig rosemary
Salt and pepper
25g / 1 oz butter, cold

- Soak the dried mushrooms in the stock while you get on with the sauce.
- Melt the butter in a pan and sweat the shallot until translucent.
- Stir in the flour to make a paste, then whisk in the red wine and cook until thickened.
- Add the mushrooms and the stock and herbs and simmer until reduced by half.
- Taste the sauce and reduce further if desired. Do not season until the sauce is the consistency you want it.
- Strain, return to the pan and whisk in the cold butter to enhance the shine. Serve.

Enriched Red wine Sauce 55

- A tbsp of cream at the end will add richness and creaminess.

56 · MAKES 500ML · Fish Stock

- Place everything in a large pan and bring to a simmer.
- Cook for 20 minutes, then strain and reserve the stock.

PREPARATION TIME 10 MINUTES

COOKING TIME 20 MINUTES

INGREDIENTS

450g / 1 lb / 2 cups fish trimmings and bones
500ml / 1 pint / 2 cups water
150ml / 5 fl oz / ⅔ cup dry white wine
1 onion, cut into quarters
2 sticks celery, chopped
Parsley sprigs
1 bay leaf
Salt and pepper

57 · SERVES 2 · Roquefort Sauce with Poppyseeds

PREPARATION TIME 5 MINUTES

COOKING TIME 10 MINUTES

INGREDIENTS

1 tbsp butter
1 shallot, finely chopped
50ml / 1 ¾ oz / ¼ cup dry white wine

300ml / 10 fl oz / 1 ¼ cups double cream
75g / 2 ½ oz / ⅓ cup Roquefort cheese
1 tsp poppyseeds
Salt and pepper

- Heat the butter in a pan and when foaming add the shallot and sweat until translucent.
- Add the wine and reduce until nearly evaporated.
- Pour in the cream and bubble up, then crumble in the cheese. Stir until melted.
- Stir in the poppyseeds and season carefully.

58 · SERVES 4 · Tomato Celery Sauce

PREPARATION TIME 10 MINUTES

COOKING TIME 30 MINUTES

INGREDIENTS

2 tbsp olive oil
1 onion, peeled and chopped
2 sticks celery, finely chopped
1 carrot, peeled and finely chopped

1 clove garlic, crushed
2 tbsp tomato puree
1 x 400g can chopped tomatoes
200ml / 7 fl oz / ¾ cup chicken stock
2 tbsp Worcestershire sauce
Pinch chilli flakes (optional)
Salt and pepper

- Heat the oil in a pan and cook the onion, celery and carrot until softened.
- Add the garlic and tomato puree and cook for 2 minutes.
- Add the tomatoes and stock and bring to a simmer. Cook for 20 minutes or until thickened and reduced.
- Whiz the sauce in a blender until smooth, then return to the pan and season with Worcestershire sauce, chilli and salt and pepper.

59

SERVES 4

Apple Sauce

PREPARATION TIME 5 MINUTES

COOKING TIME 10-15 MINUTES

....

INGREDIENTS

250g / 9 oz / 1 cup Bramley apples
250g / 9 oz / 1 cup Cox apples
1 tbsp sugar (optional, depending
on tartness of apples and usage)
2 cloves
2 tbsp water

- Peel and core the apples and cut into chunks.
- Place in a pan with the sugar, cloves and water and cover with a lid.
- Cook over a low heat for 10-15 minutes, checking occasionally, until the apples have 'exploded' to a fine puree and are soft.
- Beat to a puree, remove the cloves and serve.

Spicy Apple Sauce

60

- A pinch of mixed spice adds a kick.

61

SERVES 4

Mint Sauce

PREPARATION TIME 5 MINUTES

....

INGREDIENTS

1 bunch mint leaves
1 tbsp cider or white wine vinegar
1 tbsp olive oil
½ tsp sugar
½ tsp English mustard
Salt and pepper
3-4 tbsp natural yoghurt (optional)
1 clove of garlic, minced

- Chop the mint leaves finely and place in a food processor with the vinegar, garlic, oil, sugar and mustard.
- Whiz to make a thick sauce.
- Season and serve with roast lamb. Add the yoghurt if you want a creamier style sauce.

Garlicky Mint Sauce

62

- Adding a crushed clove garlic with the yoghurt makes this a sauce to serve with barbecued lamb.

63

SERVES 4

Béchamel Sauce

- Melt the butter in a pan, stir in the flour to make a paste.
- Whisk in the milk a bit at a time, stirring until the sauce is smooth and thick. Add the bay leaf and leave to cook for 10 minutes, stirring occasionally.
- Season and remove the bay leaf before serving.

PREPARATION TIME 5 MINUTES

COOKING TIME 15 MINUTES

INGREDIENTS

1 tbsp butter
1 tbsp plain (all purpose) flour
300ml / 10 fl oz / 1 ¼ cups milk
1 bay leaf
Salt and pepper

Mornay Sauce

64

- Add 75g/2 ½ oz grated cheddar makes this a cheese sauce for cauliflower and so on.

65

SERVES 8

Horseradish Sauce

- Peel and grate the horseradish and place in a bowl.
- Whisk in the vinegar, mustard and sugar and leave to soften for 10 minutes or so.
- Stir in the crème fraîche and season.
- This will keep for 2 days in the refrigerator.

PREPARATION TIME 20 MINUTES

INGREDIENTS

100g / 3 ½ oz / ½ cup fresh horseradish root
2 tsp red wine vinegar
1 tsp English mustard
Pinch sugar
150g / 5 oz / ⅔ cup crème fraîche
Salt and pepper

Horseradish Sauce with Capers

66

- Stir in 1 tbsp chopped rinsed capers for more of a kick.

SOUPS

Cream of Cauliflower Soup

67

SERVES 4

- Heat the butter in a pan and sweat the onion without colouring for about five minutes.
- Add the cauliflower florets and leaves, potato and garlic and cook for a further five minutes until softened.
- Add the stock and bring to the boil. Simmer for about 20 minutes until the cauliflower is completely tender.
- Liquidise in a blender, then return to the pan.
- Add the cheeses and cream and stir to melt, season carefully and reheat to serve.

PREPARATION TIME 10 MINUTES

COOKING TIME 35 MINUTES

INGREDIENTS

25g / 1 oz butter
1 onion, peeled and finely chopped
1 head cauliflower, divided into small florets, green leaves finely sliced
1 clove garlic, chopped
1 large potato, peeled and finely diced
500ml /1 pint / 2 cups vegetable stock
50g / 1 ¾ oz / ¼ cup Cheddar or blue cheese, crumbled
150ml / 5 fl. oz / ⅔ cup double cream

Indian Tomato & Lentil Soup

68

SERVES 4

PREPARATION TIME 15 MINUTES

COOKING TIME 35-40 MINUTES

INGREDIENTS

50ml / 1 ½ fl. oz / ¼ cup olive oil
1 large onion, finely chopped
2 cloves garlic, minced
3.5cm/1 inch piece of ginger, minced
1 tbsp ground coriander

2 tsp ground cumin
1 tsp Madras curry powder
½ tsp chilli powder
½ tsp turmeric
250g / 9 oz / 1 cup split lentils
4 large tomatoes, roughly chopped
1.4 l / 2 ½ pints / 5 cups vegetable stock
Coriander leaves, to garnish
Lime wedges

- Heat the olive oil in a large saucepan set over a medium heat. Sweat the onion, garlic and ginger for 6-8 minutes until soft.
- Add the ground spices and some salt and pepper. Stir well and cook for a few minutes over a reduced heat.
- Add the lentils and tomatoes, stir well then cover with the stock. Bring to the boil, skimming any scum that comes to the surface.
- Boil for 5 minutes, then reduce to simmer and cook for 20-25 minutes until the lentils have absorbed about half of the stock.
- Remove from the heat and puree roughly using a stick blender.
- Return to the heat and adjust the seasoning to taste. Ladle into serving bowls and garnish with coriander and lime wedges before serving.

Vegetable Soup

69

SERVES 4-6

PREPARATION TIME 15 MINUTES

COOKING TIME 20-25 MINUTES

INGREDIENTS

3 tbsp olive oil
1 large onion, chopped
2 carrots, roughly chopped
2 sticks celery, chopped 1 clove garlic, finely chopped

2 large potatoes, peeled and chopped
2 bay leaves
2 x 400g can chopped tomatoes
1.5L / 3 pints / 6 ⅓ cups vegetable stock
Large handful green beans, chopped
50g / 1 ¾ oz / ¼ cup peas
Salt and pepper
Extra virgin olive oil
Parmesan, to serve

- Heat the oil in a large pan and sweat the onion, carrot and celery until beginning to soften.
- Add the potatoes, garlic and bay leaves, cook for 3 minutes, then add the tomatoes and stock and bring to a simmer.
- Cook for 10 minutes then add the beans and peas and leave to simmer for another 6-7 minutes until all is tender.
- Season well.
- This soup is best served a little warmer than room temperature with extra virgin olive oil drizzled over and a generous grating of Parmesan.

70

SERVES 4

Minestrone

PREPARATION TIME 20 MINUTES

COOKING TIME I ½ HOURS

....

INGREDIENTS

2 tbsp olive oil
50g / 1 ½ oz / ⅓ cup pancetta or smoked streaky bacon
1 onion, peeled and finely chopped
2 celery stalks, finely chopped
2 carrots, peeled and finely chopped
2 cloves garlic, finely chopped
2 potatoes, peeled and finely chopped
1.5 L / 2 ½ pints / 5 cups chicken stock
200g / 6 ½ oz / ¾ cup greens, such as cavolo nero or Savoy cabbage, finely sliced
100g / 3 ½ oz / ½ cup macaroni pasta
Salt and pepper
Parmesan cheese
Extra virgin olive oil

- Heat the oil in a large pan and fry the pancetta until the fat runs and it starts to turn golden.
- Add the vegetables in the order given, giving each one a good 5 minutes to cook without colouring, stirring regularly, before adding the next one.
- Pour in the stock and bring to a gently simmer, then cook very gently for about an hour.
- Add the greens and the pasta and cook for a further 30 minutes.
- Adjust the seasoning.
- Serve hot, warm or even room temperature sprinkled with Parmesan and drizzled with olive oil.

Tomato Minestrone   71

- For a more familiar flavour, add 2 x 400g can chopped tomatoes before the stock.

72

SERVES 6

Gazpacho

PREPARATION TIME I HOUR 20 MINUTES

....

INGREDIENTS

800g / 1 ¾ lb / 3 ⅓ cups ripe tomatoes
10cm / 4 inch piece of cucumber, diced
½ bunch spring onions (scallions), finely chopped
2 cloves garlic, crushed
½ red pepper, finely chopped
1 bunch basil
100ml / 3 ½ fl oz / ½ cup extra virgin olive oil
1-2 tbsp red wine vinegar
300ml ice-cold water
Salt and pepper

FOR THE GARNISH
2 spring onions (scallions), finely chopped
10cm / 4 in piece cucumber, finely chopped
Croutons

- Cut a cross in the skin at the bottom of the tomatoes, place in a bowl of boiling water and leave for 30 seconds. This should help the skins slip off easily.
- Halve the tomatoes, deseed and chop the flesh and place in a food processor.
- Add the rest of the ingredients, then whiz until smooth.
- Pour into a bowl and adjust the seasoning if necessary.
- Chill thoroughly for at least 1 hour before serving. Check the seasoning again – it may need more as chilling dulls flavours and serve with the garnishes.

Roasted Pepper Gazpacho   73

- Roast a whole red pepper until blacked then peel carefully and process with the rest of the ingredients. This will give a sweeter, richer result.

74

SERVES 4

Pumpkin Soup with Hazelnuts

- Sweat the onion and garlic in the butter in a large pan until golden and soft.
- Add the squash and cook for five minutes, then add the thyme and stock.
- Simmer for about 20 minutes or until the squash is tender.
- Allow to cool a little, remove the thyme stems then blitz in a food processor or with a hand-held blender until smooth.
- Season and stir in the cream. Set aside.
- Toast the hazelnuts under a hot grill for a few seconds only. Sprinkle on top of the hot soup and serve.

PREPARATION TIME 10 MINUTES

COOKING TIME 40 MINUTES

....

INGREDIENTS

30g / 1oz butter
1 onion, peeled and sliced
2 garlic cloves, sliced
1 large butternut squash or pumpkin, peeled, halved, deseeded and cut into chunks
2 sprigs thyme
1 litre chicken or vegetable stock
Salt and pepper
100ml / 3 ½ fl oz / ½ cup single cream
100ml / 3 ½ fl oz / ½ cup hazelnuts (cob nuts), chopped

Pumpkin Soup with Rosemary Walnuts

75

- Toss halved walnuts in 1 tbsp finely chopped rosemary and oil and toast for a few seconds. Serve on top of the soup.

76

SERVES 4

Carrot Soup with Beetroot Crisps

- Heat the butter in a pan and sweat the onion without colouring until softened.
- Add the carrots and potato and cook for a further five minutes until softened.
- Stir in the cumin and coriander then cover with the vegetable stock. Bring to the boil and simmer for about 10 minutes until the vegetables are completely soft.
- Liquidise in a blender until smooth, then return to the pan. Add the seasoning and stir in the parsley.
- For the crisps, preheat the oven to 200°C (180° fan/ 400F / gas 7.
- Finely slice the beetroot with a vegetable peeler or on a mandolin. Toss with oil and seasoning, then lay on a baking sheet.
- Bake in the oven for 4-7 minutes, checking frequently, until golden brown.
- Serve the soup hot decorated with the beetroot crisps.

PREPARATION TIME 15 MINUTES

COOKING TIME 30 MINUTES

....

INGREDIENTS

25g / 1 oz butter
1 onion, peeled and finely chopped
500g / 1 lb / 2 cups carrots, peeled and finely chopped
1 large potato, peeled and finely diced
2 tsp ground cumin
1 tsp ground coriander
1 L / 2 ¼ pints / 4 ¼ cups vegetable stock
Salt and pepper
2 tbsp parsley, chopped
1 beetroot, peeled
Olive oil

Spicy Carrot Soup

77

- Add 1 finely chopped red chilli to the onion and carrots for a spicy twist.

78

SERVES 4

Courgette Soup

PREPARATION TIME 15 MINUTES

COOKING TIME 30-40 MINUTES

INGREDIENTS

2 tbsp olive oil
1 onion, peeled and finely chopped
2 cloves garlic, finely chopped
1 kg / 2 ¼ lb / 4 ¼ cups courgettes
(zucchini), chopped
4 sprigs thyme
1 L / 2 ¼ pints / 4 ¼ cups chicken
or vegetable stock
Salt and pepper
Squeeze of lemon juice (optional)
60ml / 2 oz / ¼ cup single cream

- Heat the oil in a large pan and sweat the onion until softened and translucent.
- Add the garlic, courgettes and thyme and cook very slowly over a low heat until the courgettes have darkened to a khaki colour and are very soft.
- Add the stock and simmer for 20 minutes.
- Liquidise ⅔ of the soup, then return to the pan, reheat and season well. Add the lemon juice if you think it needs it.
- Stir in the cream, heat gently and serve.

Chunky Courgette Soup

79

- Add a peeled, diced potato with the courgette, then when all is tender, roughly mash with a potato masher to keep the texture.

80

SERVES 4

Tomato, Pepper and Bean Soup

PREPARATION TIME 15 MINUTES

COOKING TIME 40 MINUTES

INGREDIENTS

4 tbsp olive oil
1 onion, peeled and finely sliced
2 cloves garlic, finely sliced
2 red peppers, deseeded and finely sliced
2 yellow peppers, deseeded and finely sliced
1 tbsp tomato puree
2 x 400g can chopped tomatoes
750ml / 1 ⅓ pints / 3 cups chicken or vegetable stock
2 x 400g can cannellini beans, drained
1 sprig rosemary
2 sprigs thyme
1 bay leaf
Salt and pepper
Extra virgin olive oil

- Heat the oil in a pan and cook the onion until golden.
- Add the garlic and peppers and cook until softened.
- Stir through the tomato puree and cook out for 2 minutes, then add the tomatoes, stock and beans. Throw in the herbs, bring to a simmer and cook for at least 20 minutes until rich and slightly thickened.
- If desired, crush the beans slightly with a potato masher to thicken the soup. Season well.
- Serve in deep bowls drizzled with extra virgin olive oil.

Tomato, Pepper and Bean Soup with Cured Sausage or Ham

81

- Stir in chunks of salami or slivers of cured ham for extra meaty flavour.

82

SERVES 4

Noodle Vegetable Broth

Pasta Vegetable Broth 83

- Instead of noodles, add the same amount of tiny-shaped pasta and cook in the same manner.

Noodle Squash Soup 84

- Roast cubed butternut squash in an oven until tender, then add to the soup.

Chicken and Vegetable Broth 85

- Add thinly sliced chicken breast at te same time as cooking the onion and garlic and heat until cooked through.

PREPARATION TIME 10 MINUTES

COOKING TIME 10 MINUTES

INGREDIENTS

1 tbsp groundnut oil
1 tsp sesame oil
1 red onion, peeled and finely sliced
2 cloves garlic, finely sliced
1cm piece fresh ginger, finely sliced
1 red chilli, deseeded (optional) and finely chopped
1 red pepper, deseeded and finely sliced
Handful green beans, topped and tailed
1 L / 2 ¼ pints / 4 ¼ cups chicken or vegetable stock
2 nests dried noodles
2 tbsp soy sauce
1 bunch coriander (cilantro), chopped
1 lime, juiced

- Heat the oils in a pan and sweat the onion, garlic and ginger until translucent.
- Add the chilli and vegetables and cook gently for 5 minutes or until starting to soften.
- Pour in the stock, simmer and add the noodles. Cook according to packet instructions.
- Season with the soy sauce and lime juice and sprinkle coriander over to serve.

86
SERVES 4

Parsnip Soup with Pancetta

PREPARATION TIME 10 MINUTES

COOKING TIME 35 MINUTES

....

INGREDIENTS

2 tbsp butter
1 onion, peeled and chopped
2 cloves garlic, sliced
6 parsnips, peeled and chopped
2 tsp garam masala
1 red chilli, deseeded and finely chopped
1 L / 2 ¼ pints / 4 ¼ cups vegetable stock
Salt and pepper
4 slices pancetta

- Heat the butter in a pan and cook the onion until sweet and golden.
- Add the garlic and parsnips and cook for a few minutes, then add the spices and chilli.
- Pour over the stock, bring to the boil and simmer for 20 minutes or until the parsnip is tender.
- Liquidise the soup in batches and return to the pan. Season and reheat.
- Grill the pancetta until crisp then use to decorate the soup when served.

Parsnip Soup with Parmesan   87

- Omit the pancetta and shave over parmesan for an equally meaty but vegetarian substitute.

88
SERVES 4

Cream of Tomato Soup with Basil

PREPARATION TIME 5 MINUTES

COOKING TIME 35 MINUTES

....

INGREDIENTS

500g / 1 lb / 2 cups ripe tomatoes, halved
Olive oil
Salt and pepper
Rosemary sprigs
4 cloves garlic
1 L / 2 ¼ pints / 4 ¼ cups vegetable stock
100ml / 3 ½ fl oz / ½ cup double cream
1 bunch basil leaves plus stalks

- Preheat the oven to 200°C (180° fan) / 400F / gas 7.
- Tip the tomatoes into a roasting tin and drizzle with oil. Season and tuck the rosemary and garlic cloves in and around.
- Roast in the oven until blackened and tender – about 25 minutes.
- Remove the rosemary sprigs and discard. Squeeze the garlic flesh from the skins into a blender and carefully tip in the tomatoes and their juices – you may need to do this in 2 batches – and the basil stalks.
- Add the stock and blend until smooth.
- Return the soup to a pan and heat through with the cream. Heat without boiling, then serve decorate with torn basil leaves.

Spicy Tomato Soup   89

- Stir in 1 tsp ground cumin and a large pinch dried chilli flakes for warming spice.

90

SERVES 4

Chicken, Vegetable & Basil Soup

- Heat the oil in a large pan and cook the onion, carrot and celery until softened.
- Add the garlic and potatoes and cook for 3 minutes.
- Add the chicken, turning the heat up a little and cook until golden in patches.
- Pour over the stock, add the bouquet garni and simmer gently for about 15 minutes.
- Add the peas and cook for 5 minutes.
- Season, stir in the basil and serve.

PREPARATION TIME 15 MINUTES

COOKING TIME 35 MINUTES

INGREDIENTS

2 tbsp olive oil
1 onion, peeled and finely sliced
2 sticks celery, finely chopped
2 carrots, peeled and finely chopped
1 clove garlic, crushed
2 floury potatoes, peeled and diced
4 chicken thighs, cut into fine strips
1 L / 2 ¼ pints / 4 ¼ cups chicken stock
1 bouquet garni
100g / 3 ½ oz / ½ cup frozen peas
½ bunch basil leaves
Salt and pepper

Chicken and Vegetable Noodle Soup   91

- Omit the potatoes, and instead cook noodles in the finished soup with the peas.

92

SERVES 4

Chinese Noodle Soup

- Heat the oil in a large pan and sweat the onion until translucent.
- Add the garlic, chilli slices and ginger and cook for 2 minutes, then add the remaining vegetables and cook for a few minutes.
- Pour over the stock and soy sauce and simmer for 10 minutes.
- Add the noodles and cook for about 5 minutes, until tender, then add the beansprouts.
- Adjust the seasoning and add the chilli sauce if liked.
- Serve sprinkled with fresh coriander, spring onions and a few drops of sesame oil. Add the lime slices to garnish.

PREPARATION TIME 10 MINUTES

COOKING TIME 25 MINUTES

INGREDIENTS

2 tbsp vegetable oil
1 onion, peeled and finely sliced
2 cloves garlic, finely sliced
1cm piece fresh ginger, finely sliced
2 carrots, peeled and sliced
1 courgette (zucchini), cut into matchsticks
1 red pepper, deseeded and sliced
1 yellow pepper, deseeded and sliced
1.5L / 3 pints / 6 ⅓ cups chicken or vegetable stock
3 tbsp soy sauce
2 nests dried noodles
Handful bean sprouts
Chilli sauce
Salt and pepper
2 tbsp coriander (cilantro), chopped
Sesame oil
1 red chilli, finely sliced into rings
Slices of lime, to garnish
2 spring onions, sliced diagonally

Noodle Soup with Prawns   93

- Add prawns at the same time as the onion and fry until cooked through, for a more substantial soup.

PASTA

94 · SERVES 4 · Tagliatelle Carbonara

- Cook the pasta in boiling salted water according to packet instructions.
- Heat the butter in a pan and fry the pancetta until golden.
- Whisk the egg yolks and Parmesan into the cream.
- Drain the pasta, return to the pan and, working quickly, scrape the pancetta and butter into the pan and toss.
- Toss off the heat with the egg/cream mixture then serve immediately.

PREPARATION TIME 5 MINUTES

COOKING TIME 12 MINUTES

INGREDIENTS

500g / 1lb / 2 cups tagliatelle
2 tbsp butter
12 slices pancetta or smoked streaky bacon, chopped
4 egg yolks
100ml / 3 ½ fl oz / ½ cup double cream
2 tbsp Parmesan, grated

Fresh Pasta Dough · 95 · SERVES 4

PREPARATION TIME 1 HOUR

COOKING TIME 2 MINUTES

INGREDIENTS

600g / 1 lb 6 oz / 2 ½ cups '00' flour
6 eggs or 12 egg yolks

- Tip the flour into a bowl, make a well in the centre and crack the eggs into it.
- Using a fork, beat the eggs till smooth then mix together with the flour as much as you can.
- Flour your hands and bring the dough together into a ball.
- Remove from the bowl and knead until the dough is smooth and elastic. Cover with clingfilm and leave to rest in the refrigerator for 30 minutes.
- Roll the pasta out with a pasta machine to its thinnest setting.
- Cut vertically along the strip of dough to make lasagne sheets. Set aside, lightly dusted with flour until ready to use.

Spaghetti Bolognese · 96 · SERVES 4

PREPARATION TIME 15 MINUTES

COOKING TIME 40 MINUTES

INGREDIENTS

500g / 1 lb / 2 cups spaghetti
3 tbsp olive oil
2 onions, peeled and finely chopped
2 cloves garlic, chopped
1 pack pancetta or bacon lardons
500g / 1 lb / 2 cups minced beef
100g / 3 ½ oz / ½ cup chicken livers, finely chopped
1 glass dry white wine
2 x 400g can chopped tomatoes
4 tbsp double cream
100g / 3 ½ oz / ½ cup Parmesan, grated
1 bunch parsley, chopped
Salt and pepper

- Heat the oil in a pan and sweat the onion and garlic without colouring.
- Add the pancetta and fry until the fat runs.
- Add the mince and break it up with a wooden spoon, stirring frequently until browned.
- Add the chicken livers and cook until browned all over.
- Season, then add the wine, bubble up, then add the tomatoes. Partially cover and simmer for 20 minutes.
- Meanwhile cook the pasta in boiling salted water according to packet instructions. Drain and toss with a little oil.
- Stir the cream and parsley through the sauce, then toss the pasta in the sauce.

97

SERVES 4

Spiral Pasta with Tricolore Sauce

PREPARATION TIME 5 MINUTES

COOKING TIME 12 MINUTES

500g / 1 lb / 2 cups spirali pasta
2 tbsp olive oil
1 clove garlic, finely sliced
2 x 400g can plum tomatoes
1 bunch basil
1 ball mozzarella
2 tbsp pitted black olives, chopped
Salt and pepper

- Cook the pasta in boiling salted water according to packet instructions.
- Meanwhile heat the olive oil in a pan until quite hot, throw in the garlic and the whole tomatoes without the juice. Cover with a lid as it will spit.
- When the spitting dies down, remove the lid and break down the tomatoes. Stir in the basil, season and remove from the heat.
- Drain the pasta and toss with the sauce.
- Stir in chunks of mozzarella and the chopped olives and serve.

Tricolore Pasta with Basil Oil — 98

- Instead of stirring the basil into the sauce, simply whizz in a blender with a few tbsp olive oil until smooth then drizzle over the dish.

99

SERVES 6

Lasagne Bolognese

PREPARATION TIME 2 HOURS

COOKING TIME 40 MINUTES

INGREDIENTS

12 sheets of lasagne (see page 51)
4 tbsp of Parmesan cheese

FOR THE BOLOGNESE SAUCE
1 tbsp butter
Olive oil
1 onion, peeled and finely chopped
2 celery stalks, finely chopped
2 cloves garlic, finely chopped
2 carrots, finely chopped
120g / 4 oz / ½ cup pancetta, cubed
500g / 1 lb minced beef
120ml / 4 fl oz / ½ cup white wine
2 x 400g can chopped tomatoes
450ml / 1 pint / 2 cups beef stock
Salt and pepper

FOR THE BÉCHAMEL SAUCE
See page 31.

- Make the Bolognese sauce: heat the butter with a little oil in a pan and add the finely chopped vegetables, the carrots and pancetta and cook for about 10 minutes.
- Add the beef, breaking it up with a wooden spoon until cooked through. Season.
- Add the wine and stir for about 5 minutes until it has been absorbed. Add the tomatoes and half the stock and then lower the heat. Partially cover the pan and leave to simmer for about 1 ½ - 2 hours, adding more stock as it absorbs. Don't let it get too thick.
- Meanwhile, make the béchamel sauce (see page 31).
- Preheat the oven to 190°C / 375F / gas 5. Spread a third of the Bolognese sauce in the bottom of a baking dish, then a quarter of the béchamel, then 4 sheets of lasagne.
- Repeat twice more, then cover the top layer of lasagne with béchamel and sprinkle over the parmesan.
- Bake in the oven for about 40 minutes.

Lasagne Bolognese with Spinach — 100

- Wilt 3 large handfuls of spinach and spread over the pasta before adding the sauce.

Spinach & Ricotta Cannelloni

101

SERVES 4

- Preheat the oven to 180°C / 350F / gas 5.
- Make the filling: heat the butter in a large pan with a little oil and cook the garlic for 2 minutes. Add the spinach and nutmeg and stir until wilted.
- Spoon into a sieve and press down firmly with a wooden spoon to extract as much liquid as possible. Once done, finely chop the spinach and leave to cool in a bowl.
- Stir in the ricotta, Parmesan and seasoning.
- Spoon into the tubes or onto the lasagne sheets and roll up to make 12 cylinders, then lay in a greased baking dish.
- Make the tomato sauce: heat the oil in a pan and add the garlic and tomatoes. Leave to simmer, topped up with ½ a can of water, for 10 minutes, then add the basil.
- Spoon over the cannelloni and bake for around 15 minutes until bubbling.

Spinach Mascarpone Cannelloni
102

- Substitute mascarpone for the ricotta for a creamier sauce, adding 2 tbsp grated Parmesan for flavour.

PREPARATION TIME 40 MINUTES

COOKING TIME 15 MINUTES

INGREDIENTS

12 cannelloni tubes or 12 sheets lasagne (see page 51)

FOR THE FILLING
2 tbsp butter
Olive oil
2 cloves garlic, chopped
¼ nutmeg, grated
1 kg / 2 lb / 4 ½ cups spinach leaves
400g / 13 ½ oz / 1 ½ cups ricotta
2 tbsp Parmesan, grated
Salt and pepper

FOR THE TOMATO SAUCE
2 tbsp olive oil
1 clove garlic, chopped
2 x 400g can chopped tomatoes
½ bunch basil, chopped

Meat Cannelloni

103

SERVES 4

- Preheat the oven to 190°C / 375F / gas 5.
- Make the filling: heat the butter with a little oil and cook the vegetables until soft.
- Add the beef and pork break it down with a wooden spoon, stirring until it is cooked through.
- Add the white wine and season and allow the wine to evaporate.
- Use a teaspoon to fill the cannelloni tubes with the beef mixture then lay in a greased baking dish.
- Lay the mozzarella slices over the pasta and smear with the tomato puree or passata.
- Bake in the oven for 10-15 minutes until bubbling and golden.

Meat Cannelloni with Tomato Sauce
104

- Before adding the mozzarella, top with tomato sauce, as in the recipe above.

PREPARATION TIME 20 MINUTES

COOKING TIME 10-15 MINUTES

INGREDIENTS

12 cannelloni tubes or 12 sheets of lasagne (see page 51)
2 balls mozzarella, sliced

FOR THE FILLING
1 tbsp butter
Olive oil
1 onion, peeled and finely chopped
2 celery stalks, finely chopped
2 cloves garlic, finely chopped
2 carrots, finely chopped
250g / ½ lb minced beef
250g / ½ lb minced pork
120ml / 4 fl oz / ½ cup dry white wine
3 tbsp tomato puree or passata
Salt and pepper

105

SERVES 2

Tortelloni in Creamy Tomato Sauce

Tortelloni in Tomato Sauce

106

- Omit the mascarpone if you're counting calories.

Tortelloni with Tomato Pancetta Sauce

107

- Add 50g 1 ¾ oz cubed pancetta to the pan with the onion.

Tortelloni with Tomato Mozzarella Sauce

108

- Stirring cubed mozzarella into the sauce just before serving makes it deliciously oozing and stringy.

PREPARATION TIME 5 MINUTES

COOKING TIME 15 MINUTES

INGREDIENTS

1 x pack fresh-made tortelloni, such as ham and cheese or spinach and ricotta

FOR THE SAUCE
2 tbsp olive oil
1 onion, finely chopped
1 clove garlic, finely chopped
1 x 400g can chopped tomatoes
Handful thyme leaves
100ml / 3 ½ oz / ½ cup mascarpone
Salt and pepper

- Heat the oil in a pan and sweat the onion and garlic without colouring.
- Add the tomatoes and a splash of water and simmer for 10 minutes, then stir in the thyme leaves and mascarpone and season.
- Cook the pasta in boiling salted water according to packet instructions. Drain.
- Toss the pasta with the sauce and serve.

109

SERVES 4

Penne with Ham & Cream Sauce

- Cook the pasta in boiling salted water according to packet instructions.
- Drain, hiving off a cupful of the cooking water and reserve.
- Meanwhile heat the butter in a pan and sweat the onion and garlic till translucent.
- Add the chopped ham and cream, season and add a little grated nutmeg.
- Toss the pasta into the cream sauce with a little of the cooking water to loosen.
- Serve sprinkled with parsley and parmesan.

PREPARATION TIME 5 MINUTES

COOKING TIME 15-20 MINUTES

INGREDIENTS

500g / 1 lb / 2 cups penne pasta
1 tbsp butter
½ onion, peeled and finely chopped
1 clove garlic, finely sliced
3 thick slices ham, chopped
300ml / 10 fl oz / 1 ¼ cups double cream
Salt and pepper
Grated nutmeg
½ bunch parsley, chopped
Parmesan, grated

Penne with Mushroom Sauce

110

- For meaty flavour without the ham, simply stir in a large handful quartered chestnut mushrooms with the butter until golden.

111

SERVES 4

Papardelle in Creamy Chive Sauce

- Cook the pasta in boiling salted water according to packet instructions.
- Drain thoroughly after hiving off a cupful of the cooking water.
- Heat the mascarpone in a pan with the chives, a little lemon juice and seasoning.
- Add the pasta and a little cooking water to loosen, toss well and serve.

PREPARATION TIME 5 MINUTES

COOKING TIME 10 MINUTES

INGREDIENTS

400g / 13 ½ oz / 1 ½ cups pappardelle pasta
225g / 8 oz / 1 cup mascarpone
½ bunch chives, chopped
Squeeze of lemon juice
Salt and pepper

Pappardelle with Creamy Cheese Chive Sauce

112

- Stir in 50g / 1 ¾ oz grated gruyere or parmesan.

(113)

SERVES 4

Asparagus Tagliatelle

PREPARATION TIME 10 MINUTES

COOKING TIME 12 MINUTES

INGREDIENTS

500g / 1 lb / 2 cups tagliatelle pasta
½ bunch asparagus, woody ends
snapped off and cut into short
lengths
60g / 2 oz / ¼ cup butter
1 clove garlic, sliced
¼ lemon, grated zest
Salt and pepper

- Cook the pasta in boiling salted water according to packet instructions.
- Add the asparagus 3 minutes before the end of the cooking time.
- Meanwhile heat the butter and garlic in a pan, then add the zest and toss together.
- Drain the pasta, reserving a little of the water and toss with the butter sauce, adding 1-2 tbsp of reserved cooking water to amalgamate the sauce.
- Season and serve.

Asparagus and Broad Bean Tagliatelle

(114)

- Add 60g / 2 oz double podded cooked broad beans to the pasta.

(115)

SERVES 4-6

Tagliatelle with Meatballs

PREPARATION TIME 50 MINUTES

COOKING TIME 30 MINUTES

INGREDIENTS

350g / 12 oz / 1 ⅓ cups tagliatelle
Parmesan, grated to serve

FOR THE MEATBALLS
400g / 14 oz / 1 ½ cups minced beef
1 egg
2 tbsp parsley, chopped
1 clove garlic, crushed
½ lemon, grated zest
Salt and pepper
1 thick slice of white bread, crusts
removed soaked in 2 tbsp milk
3 tbsp olive oil
1 x 400g can chopped tomatoes
400ml / 14 fl oz / 1 ½ cups beef stock
1 tsp sugar

- Place the meat in a large bowl with the egg, garlic, lemon zest and 1 tbsp parsley and season.
- Mulch the bread in your fingers and crumble into the mix. Mix everything together with your hands to become smooth and sticky.
- Roll into small walnut-sized balls with cold wet hands, place on a tray and chill for 30 minutes.
- Heat the oil in a pan and fry the meatballs in batches until brown.
- Add the tomatoes and stock, then add the sugar and season and bring to the boil. Lower the heat and simmer for about 20 minutes.
- Meanwhile cook the pasta in boiling salted water according to packet instructions.
- Drain and tip into a large bowl. Pour the sauce over the pasta, sprinkle over the parsley and Parmesan and serve.

Tagliatelle with Lamb Meatballs

(116)

- Substitute minced lamb for the beef and add ½ tsp ground cinnamon and 1 tsp ground cumin to the mixture.

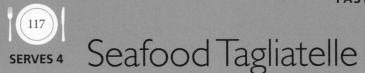

SERVES 4 Seafood Tagliatelle

Tagliatelle with Squid   118

- Try adding thawed squid rings in with the seafood.

Tagliatelle with Dill Aioli   119

- Stir chopped dill into the aioli recipe on P26 and serve on top of the seafood tagliatelle.

Seafood Tagliatelle a Bianco   120

- Omit the canned tomatoes, but use a glass of dry white wine and reduce by a third before adding the seafood and cooking juices.

PREPARATION TIME 15 MINUTES

COOKING TIME 15-20 MINUTES

INGREDIENTS

500g / 1 lb / 2 cups tagliatelle
2 tbsp olive oil
1 shallot, finely chopped
2 cloves garlic, finely chopped
Pinch dried chilli flakes
1 x 400g can tomatoes
2 sprigs thyme
200g / 7 oz / ¾ cup raw prawns
(shrimp), shelled
8 scallops, sliced in half horizontally
250g / 9 oz / 1 cup mussels, cleaned
Salt and pepper

- Cook the pasta in boiling salted water according to packet instructions. Drain the pasta and toss with a little oil.
- Heat the oil in a pan and sweat the shallot and garlic with chilli flakes without colouring.
- Add the tomatoes with a splash of water and leave to simmer for 10 minutes.
- Meanwhile, cook the mussels in a separate pan with a splash of water for about 5 minutes or until they have opened. Discard any that remain closed.
- Drain over a bowl to catch the cooking juices. Remove the meat from the mussels once cool.
- Add the thyme, prawns and scallops to the tomato mixture and leave to cook until the prawns are pink and the scallops just opaque.
- Add the mussels and a little of their cooking liquor and season. Toss the tagliatelle through the sauce and serve.

121

SERVES 4

Spaghetti with Red Pesto

Spaghetti with Green Pesto

122

- Make the green pesto sauce as on page 23 and use as above.

Spaghetti with Red Pesto Mascarpone Sauce

123

- Stir 3 tbsp mascarpone into the sauce for a creamy result.

Spaghetti Tricolore

124

- For a real shot of colour, stir wilted spinach through the spaghetti before topping with the pesto.

PREPARATION TIME 5 MINUTES

COOKING TIME 10 MINUTES

INGREDIENTS

500g / 1 lb / 2 cups spaghetti
Parmesan, grated to serve

FOR THE PESTO SAUCE
Small handful pine nuts
1 clove garlic, peeled and chopped
250g / 9 oz / 1 cup sun-dried or demi-sec tomatoes, drained
½ red chilli, deseeded and finely chopped
2 tbsp parsley, chopped
2 tbsp Parmesan, grated
Extra virgin olive oil

- Cook the pasta in boiling salted water according to packet instructions. Drain, reserving a little of the cooking water.
- Make the pesto sauce: Whiz all of the ingredients in a food processor until you have a rough paste or pound in a pestle and mortar. Drizzle in enough oil to make a loose sauce.
- Toss the pasta in the pesto, loosening with a little cooking water.
- Serve with extra Parmesan.

125
SERVES 4

Farfalle with Summer Vegetables

- Cook the pasta in boiling salted water according to packet instructions.
- 4 minutes before the end of cooking, add the peas. When cooked, drain, reserving a cupful of cooking water and toss with a little oil.
- Meanwhile drizzle the tomatoes with oil, toss with the garlic and seasoning and leave to macerate.
- Heat the oil in a pan and quickly cook the courgette until golden and tender.
- Toss the hot pasta with the peas, macerated tomatoes and courgette and a little reserved cooking water and top with pesto to serve.

PREPARATION TIME 10 MINUTES

COOKING TIME 12-15 MINUTES

....

INGREDIENTS

500g / 1lb/ 2 cups farfalle pasta
100g / 3 ½ oz / ½ cup peas
16 ripe cherry tomatoes, halved
½ clove garlic, crushed
Extra virgin olive oil
Salt and pepper
2 tbsp olive oil
1 courgette (zucchini), finely diced
4 tbsp pesto

Farfalle with Winter Vegetables

126

- Use shredded savoy cabbage or cavolo nero in place of the peas and courgette.

127
SERVES 4

Gnocchi in Tomato Sauce with Basil

- Boil the potatoes whole and unpeeled in boiling salted water for at least 25 minutes until completely tender.
- Drain and mash thoroughly.
- Heat the oil in a pan and fry the garlic gently, then add the tomatoes with a splash of water. Simmer for 10 minutes, then season and stir in the basil.
- Tip the cooled potatoes into a bowl and work in the flour, egg, a pinch of salt and nutmeg until you have a smooth dough. Cut the dough in half and roll out to make 2 fat sausages.
- Cut into pieces about 3cm long and press down gently with the tines of a fork to make the traditional indentations. Place on a floured baking sheet to cook when ready.
- To cook the gnocchi, bring a large pan of salted water to the boil then add the gnocchi. When they float to the top, they are ready. Remove and drain and toss with the tomato sauce and serve.

PREPARATION TIME 1 HOUR

COOKING TIME 5 MINUTES

....

INGREDIENTS

700g floury potatoes, such as Maris Piper
250g plain (all-purpose) flour
1 egg, beaten
Salt
Nutmeg

FOR THE TOMATO SAUCE
2 tbsp olive oil
1 clove garlic, finely chopped
1 x 400g can tomatoes
½ bunch basil, chopped
Salt and pepper

Baked Gnocchi with Tomato Sauce

128

- Tip into a gratin dish, top with slices of mozzarella and bake until melted and oozing.

RICE AND NOODLES

129

SERVES 4

Paella

- Heat the olive oil in a large shallow pan and cook the onion, garlic and celery with the chorizo until the orange fat runs.
- Add the pepper, cook for a further 5 minutes, then stir in the chicken and paella rice and coat thoroughly in the oil.
- Stir the saffron into the stock then pour it over the rice. Add the paprika. Bring to a simmer and leave uncovered for 10 minutes.
- Add the tomatoes, peas and seafood and cook for a further 8-10 minutes until everything is just cooked through and the mussels have opened.
- Stir through the lemon juice, season well and serve.

PREPARATION TIME 20 MINUTES

COOKING TIME 30 MINUTES

INGREDIENTS

5 tbsp olive oil
1 onion, peeled and finely sliced
75g / 2 ½ oz / ⅓ cup chorizo, diced
2 cloves garlic, finely chopped
1 celery stick, finely chopped
1 red pepper, seeded and sliced
300g / 10 oz / 1 ¼ cups paella rice
2 chicken thighs, cubed
1L / 2 ¼ pints / 4 ¼ cups chicken stock
Pinch saffron threads
1 tsp paprika
4 ripe tomatoes, chopped
50g / 1 ¾ oz / ¼ cup frozen peas
12 raw prawns (shrimp), shell on
24 mussels, cleaned
2 fillets chunky white fish, skinned, boned and cubed
1 lemon, juiced
Salt and pepper

130

SERVES 4

Pilau Rice

PREPARATION TIME 30 MINUTES

COOKING TIME 15 MINUTES

INGREDIENTS

500g / 1lb/ 2 cups basmati rice
30g / 1 oz butter
1 onion, peeled and finely chopped

5 cardamom pods, lightly crushed
1 cinnamon stick
6 cloves
Pinch saffron soaked in 500ml / 1 pint / 2 cups vegetable stock
Salt

- Wash the rice in a sieve under cold running water, then leave to soak for 30 minutes.
- Heat the butter in a pan and when foaming add the onion. Cook until golden and sweet.
- Add the spices and toast lightly, then tip in the rice and stir well to coat in the butter.
- Pour over the stock and a little salt, bring to the boil and cover with a lid. Turn the heat down and leave to cook for 9-10 minutes.
- Turn off the heat and leave to stand for 5 minutes. Remove the lid and stir with a fork to separate the grains.

131

SERVES 2

Vermicelli Chive Paillasson

PREPARATION TIME 5 MINUTES

COOKING TIME 6 MINUTES

INGREDIENTS

150g / 5 oz / ⅔ cup rice vermicelli
1 bunch chives, chopped
1 egg

Salt and pepper
1 tsp sesame oil
1 tbsp groundnut oil

- Soak the vermicelli in boiling water to soften.
- After 30-60 seconds, drain thoroughly and snip into pieces.
- Mix with the chives and egg and season. Form into rough patties.
- Heat the oil in a pan and when hot, fry the patties on both sides for a couple of minute until golden.
- Drain briefly on kitchen paper and serve.

Cep risotto

Cep and Red Wine Risotto 133

- Use red wine instead of white for a dramatic colour variation.

Cep and Parsley Risotto 134

- Stir in ½ bunch chopped parsley at the end of cooking.

Cep and Ham Risotto 135

- Some finely chopped ham will add depth of flavour.

PREPARATION TIME 10 MINUTES

COOKING TIME 25 MINUTES

INGREDIENTS

2 tbsp olive oil
40g / 1 oz butter
1 onion, peeled and finely chopped
2 cloves garlic, finely chopped
200g / 7 oz / ¾ cup ceps or other wild mushrooms
1 tbsp thyme leaves
320g / 11 oz / 1 ⅓ cups risotto rice
100ml / 3 ½ fl oz / ½ cup dry white wine
1L / 2 ¼ pints / 4 ¼ cups chicken or vegetable stock
Salt and pepper
3 tbsp butter
120g / 4 oz / ½ cup Parmesan, grated

- Heat the oil and butter in a large pan and add the onion and garlic. Cook until soft and translucent.
- Stir in the torn mushrooms and thyme and cook for a few minutes.
- Add the rice and stir to coat in the butter. Pour in the wine and stir the rice while the wine is absorbed.
- Once the wine has cooked in, reduce the heat a little and add the hot stock, a ladleful at a time, stirring fairly continuously. This will give the risotto its creamy texture.
- Keep stirring in the stock and tasting the rice. After about 15-20 minutes the rice should be soft but with a slight bite. If you've run out of stock before the rice is cooked, simply use water.
- Season and remove from the heat. Add the butter and Parmesan (mantecatura) and leave to melt into the risotto. Serve immediately.

136
SERVES 4
Asparagus Risotto

- Heat the oil and butter in a large pan and add the onion and garlic. Cook until soft and translucent.
- Chop the asparagus into short lengths and add to the pan. Cook for a few minutes.
- Add the rice and stir to coat in the butter. Pour in the wine and stir the rice while the wine is absorbed.
- Once the wine has cooked in, reduce the heat a little and add the hot stock, a ladleful at a time, stirring fairly continuously. This will give the risotto its creamy texture.
- Keep stirring in the stock and tasting the rice. After about 15-20 minutes the rice should be soft but with a slight bite. If you've run out of stock before the rice is cooked, simply use water.
- Season and remove from the heat. Add the butter and Parmesan (mantecatura) and leave to melt into the risotto. Stir in the lemon zest and juice.

Asparagus and Pea Risotto
137
- A handful of peas cooked in the risotto add sweetness.

PREPARATION TIME 10 MINUTES

COOKING TIME 25 MINUTES

INGREDIENTS

2 tbsp olive oil
40g / 1 oz butter
1 onion, peeled and finely chopped
1 bunch asparagus, woody ends snapped off
320g / 11 oz / 1 ⅓ cups risotto rice
100ml / 3 ½ fl oz / ½ cup dry white wine
1L / 2 ¼ pints / 4 ¼ cups chicken or vegetable stock
Salt and pepper
3 tbsp butter
120g / 4 oz / ½ cup Parmesan, grated
1 lemon, juiced and grated zest

138
SERVES 4
Pancetta & Parmesan Risotto

- Heat the oil and butter in a large pan and add the onion and garlic. Cook until soft and translucent.
- Add the pancetta and cook until golden.
- Add the rice and stir to coat in the butter. Pour in the wine and stir the rice while the wine is absorbed.
- Once the wine has cooked in, reduce the heat a little and add the hot stock, a ladleful at a time, stirring fairly continuously. This will give the risotto its creamy texture.
- Keep stirring in the stock and tasting the rice. After about 15-20 minutes the rice should be soft but with a slight bite. If you've run out of stock before the rice is cooked, simply use water.
- Season and remove from the heat. Add the butter and Parmesan (mantecatura) and leave to melt into the risotto. Serve immediately.

Pancetta Vegetable Risotto
139
- Peas, spinach and asparagus, all cooked in the risotto would complement the smoky pancetta.

PREPARATION TIME 10 MINUTES

COOKING TIME 25 MINUTES

INGREDIENTS

2 tbsp olive oil
40g /1 oz butter
1 onion, peeled and finely chopped
2 cloves garlic, finely chopped
150g pancetta, cubed
320g / 11 oz / 1 ⅓ cups risotto rice
100ml / 3 ½ fl oz / ½ cup dry white wine
1L / 2 ¼ pints / 4 ¼ cups chicken or vegetable stock
Salt and pepper
3 tbsp butter
120g / 4 oz / ½ cup Parmesan, grated

SERVES 4

Noodles with Salmon, Peas & Broccoli

Noodles with Fresh Tuna
141

- Substitute fresh tuna steaks for the salmon.

Noodles with Salmon and Mustard Sauce
142

- Mix together 1 tsp English mustard powder with the soy and toss with the noodles for an anglo-oriental take.

Noodles with Salmon, Peas and Broccoli
143

- Use asparagus lengths rather than broccoli.

PREPARATION TIME 10 MINUTES

COOKING TIME 10 MINUTES

INGREDIENTS

4 nests dried noodles
1 head broccoli, cut into florets
100g / 3 ½ oz / ½ cup frozen peas
1 tbsp groundnut oil
4 spring onions (scallions), finely chopped
1cm piece ginger, finely sliced
2 salmon fillets, boned and cut into strips
2 tbsp soy sauce
2 tbsp chilli sauce
1 tsp sesame oil

- Cook the noodles in boiling salted water according to packet instructions.
- After 1 minute add the broccoli and peas.
- Drain well.
- Meanwhile heat the oil in a wok and add the spring onions and ginger. Sauté for a few minutes, then add the salmon and cook until just pink.
- Add the noodles and vegetables and pour in the sauces.
- Toss well to coat, then serve drizzled with sesame oil.

144
SERVES: 4

Arancini with Tomato and Mozzarella

- Leave the leftover risotto to get completely cold – preferably refrigerated overnight.
- Stir the tomato and Parmesan through the risotto.
- Shape into equal balls, pushing a small cube of mozzarella into the centre of each one and shaping the rice around it. If you prefer, you could make finger shapes instead.
- Lay out the flour, egg and breadcrumbs on separate plates.
- Dip the risotto balls into the flour, then the egg, then the breadcrumbs. Use one hand and keep the other clean for ease.
- Heat the oil to 180°C or until a cube of bread sizzles when dunked in. Fry the risotto balls until golden and crisp all over. Drain on kitchen paper and serve hot or warm.

PREPARATION TIME 20 MINUTES

COOKING TIME 10 MINUTES

INGREDIENTS

60g / 2 oz / ¼ cup leftover risotto rice, cooked
1 tbsp Parmesan, grated
1 tomato, seeded and finely diced
1 ball mozzarella, cut into small cubes
½ bunch basil leaves
1 tbsp plain (all purpose) flour
1 egg, beaten
40g / 1 ½ oz breadcrumbs
Vegetable oil, for deep frying

Blue Cheese Arancini   145

- Omit the tomato and use gorgonzola instead of the mozzarella.

146
SERVES 4

Saffron Risotto

- Heat the oil and butter in a large pan and add the onion and garlic. Cook until soft and translucent.
- Add the rice and stir to coat in the butter. Pour in the wine and stir the rice while the wine is absorbed.
- Once the wine has cooked in, reduce the heat a little and add the hot stock, a ladleful at a time, stirring fairly continuously. This will give the risotto its creamy texture.
- Keep stirring in the stock and tasting the rice. After about 15-20 minutes the rice should be soft but with a slight bite. If you've run out of stock before the rice is cooked, simply use water.
- Season and remove from the heat. Add the butter and Parmesan (mantecatura) and leave to melt into the risotto. Serve immediately.

PREPARATION TIME 5 MINUTES

COOKING TIME 25 MINUTES

INGREDIENTS

2 tbsp olive oil
40g / 1 oz butter
1 onion, peeled and finely chopped
2 cloves garlic, finely chopped
320g / 11 oz / 1 ⅓ cups risotto rice
100ml / 3 ½ fl oz / ½ cup dry white wine
1 L / 2 ¼ pints / 4 ¼ cups chicken or vegetable stock with pinch saffron threads soaking
Salt and pepper
3 tbsp butter
120g / 4 oz / ½ cup Parmesan, grated

Saffron Risotto with Mushrooms   147

- Add 100g / 3 ½ oz chopped mushrooms with the onion for earthy flavour.

148

SERVES 2

Noodles with Chorizo & Peas

PREPARATION TIME 5 MINUTES

COOKING TIME 10 MINUTES

....

INGREDIENTS

2 nests dried noodles
100g / 3 ½ oz / ½ cup frozen peas
1 tbsp groundnut oil
100g / 3 ½ oz / ½ cup chorizo
sausage, sliced
½ red onion, peeled and finely sliced
1 red chilli, finely sliced

- Cook the noodles according to packet instructions along with the peas.
- Drain and set aside.
- Meanwhile heat the oil in a pan and fry the chorizo and onion until the fat runs and the onion is soft.
- Toss in the noodles and peas then add the chilli.
- Serve.

Noodles with Chicken and Peas   149

- Use leftover shredded roast chicken if you don't have chorizo.

150

SERVES 4

Tomato, Pepper and Mushroom Risotto

PREPARATION TIME 15 MINUTES

COOKING TIME 25 MINUTES

....

INGREDIENTS

2 tbsp olive oil
40g / 1 oz butter
1 onion, peeled and finely chopped
2 cloves garlic, finely chopped
100g / 3 ½ oz / ½ cup button
mushrooms, sliced
1 red pepper, deseeded and finely
chopped
150g cherry tomatoes, halved
320g / 11 oz / 1 ⅓ cups risotto rice
100ml / 3 ½ fl oz / ½ cup dry white
wine
1 L / 2 ¼ pints / 4 ¼ cups chicken or
vegetable stock
Salt and pepper
3 tbsp butter
120g / 4 oz / ½ cup Parmesan, grated

- Heat the oil and butter in a large pan and add the onion and garlic. Cook until soft and translucent.
- Add the mushrooms and cook until lightly golden then add the pepper and cook for a few minutes.
- Add the rice and stir to coat in the butter. Pour in the wine and stir the rice while the wine is absorbed.
- Once the wine has cooked in, reduce the heat a little and add the hot stock, a ladleful at a time, stirring fairly continuously. This will give the risotto its creamy texture.
- Keep stirring in the stock and tasting the rice. After about 15-20 minutes the rice should be soft but with a slight bite. If you've run out of stock before the rice is cooked, simply use water.
- Season and remove from the heat. Add the butter and Parmesan and leave to melt into the risotto. Serve immediately.

Tomato Red Pepper Courgette Risotto   151

- Omit the mushrooms and use 1 diced courgette.

SERVES 4 Noodles with Pork & Lemongrass

With Caramelised Chicken 153

- Use chicken instead of pork.

With Caramelised Tofu 154

- Use cubed tofu instead of pork.

Noodle Broth with Pork 155

- Cook the noodles in 500ml/1 pint strong chicken stock, then pour the stock into bowls and serve the noodles and pork on top.

PREPARATION TIME 15 MINUTES

COOKING TIME 10 MINUTES

....

INGREDIENTS

4 nests dried noodles
1 small red onion, finely sliced
2 tbsp groundnut oil
2 cloves garlic, finely sliced
1cm piece ginger, finely sliced
1 red chilli, deseeded and finely chopped
2 stalks lemongrass, inner stalks only, finely chopped
300g / 10 oz / pork fillet, cubed
2 tbsp sugar
1 tbsp soy sauce

- Cook the noodles according to packet instructions. Drain.
- Heat the oil in a wok and sauté the garlic, onion, ginger and chilli with the lemongrass for a few minutes until golden.
- Add the pork and colour over a high heat, then add the sugar and soy and allow to caramelize.
- Add the noodles and toss well to heat through.

POTATOES

156

SERVES 2

Potato Omelette

- Cut the potatoes into dice and cook in boiling salted water until tender. Drain thoroughly and set aside.
- Meanwhile crack the eggs into a bowl and beat lightly. Tip into the pan and swirl gently to cover the base of the pan and help it set.
- When the omelette is nearly set, sprinkle over the potatoes, parsley and seasoning and flash under a hot grill to set it completely.
- Remove from the pan and serve.

PREPARATION TIME 15 MINUTES

COOKING TIME 5 MINUTES

INGREDIENTS

250g / 9 oz / 1 cup potatoes, peeled
1 tbsp butter
2 eggs
Salt and pepper
2 tbsp parsley, chopped

Potato Dauphinoise

157

SERVES 4-6

PREPARATION TIME 20 MINUTES

COOKING TIME 1 ½ - 2 HOURS

INGREDIENTS

50g / 1 ¾ oz butter, softened
1 kg / 2 ¼ lb / 4 ¼ cups floury potatoes, peeled
2 cloves garlic, crushed

Salt and pepper
½ bunch thyme
500ml / 1 pint / 2 cups double cream
Milk

- Preheat oven to 160°C (140° fan) / 300F / gas 2.
- Use the softened butter to generously grease a large baking dish.
- Slice the potatoes as thinly as possible – about as thin as a coin, using either a sharp knife or, preferably a mandoline.
- Layer the potatoes in the baking dish, seasoning and sprinkling with thyme leaves and garlic as you go.
- Pour the cream over the potatoes – it should come just to the top of the potatoes. If you don't have enough, just add some milk.
- Push the potatoes down into the cream, place on a baking sheet and bake for 1 ½ - 2 hours until the potatoes are completely tender all the way through and the gratin is golden and bubbling.
- Leave for 5 minutes to settle before serving.

Sweet Potato Mash

158

SERVES 4

PREPARATION TIME 5 MINUTES

COOKING TIME 15 MINUTES

INGREDIENTS

4 large sweet potatoes, peeled
Salt
50g / 1 ¾ oz butter
Pepper

- Cut the potatoes into large chunks and cook in boiling salted water until tender – about 10-12 minutes.
- Drain thoroughly, then set the pan over a low heat and shake the pan to drive off any excess moisture.
- Mash thoroughly with the butter until smooth then season generously and serve.

159

SERVES 4

Griddled Sweet Potato

PREPARATION TIME 10 MINUTES

COOKING TIME 8-10 MINUTES

INGREDIENTS

2 large sweet potatoes, scrubbed
4 tbsp olive oil
Pinch dried chilli flakes (optional)
2 sprigs thyme leaves
Salt and pepper

- Cut the potatoes across into thick rounds about 2cm thick.
- Rub with oil, chilli, thyme and season and score a cross-hatch into each side to help them cook quickly.
- Heat a griddle pan or barbecue until very hot then cook the potato slices until golden on both sides and tender all the way through – about 8-10 minutes per side, turning them regularly to prevent burning.

Griddled Potatoes 160

- You can sue this method with ordinary white potatoes as well.

161

SERVES 4

Baked Potatoes with Cottage Cheese

PREPARATION TIME 10 MINUTES

COOKING TIME 1 HOUR 10

MINUTES – 1 HOUR 40 MINUTES

INGREDIENTS

4 large baking potatoes, such as King Edward or Maris Piper, scrubbed
2 tbsp olive oil
Salt

FOR THE FILLING
250g / 9 oz / 1 cup cottage cheese
1 tbsp thyme leaves
1 tbsp parsley, chopped
2 tbsp chives, chopped
Salt and pepper
Squeeze of lemon juice
3 tbsp extra virgin olive oil

- Preheat the oven to 200°C / 400F / gas 7.
- Rub the potatoes all over with olive oil, prick the skins a few times with a fork and sprinkle generously with salt. Bake in the oven for at least 1 hour until completely cooked.
- Meanwhile mix together the ingredients for the filling and chill.
- Once the potatoes are cooked, split them in half and spoon the cold filling into the hot potatoes.

Stuffed with Herby Sour Cream 162

- Sour cream is a surprisingly delicious accompaniment, worth revisiting with the same mixture of herbs.

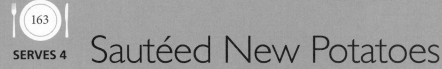

163
SERVES 4

Sautéed New Potatoes

New Potatoes with Rosemary
164

- Use finely chopped rosemary rather than thyme.

New Potatoes with Smoky Bacon
165

- Use 4 rashers chopped smoked streaky bacon for a punch.

New Potatoes with Wild Mushrooms
166

- Saute wild mushrooms with the potatoes.

PREPARATION TIME 10 MINUTES

COOKING TIME 10-15 MINUTES

....

INGREDIENTS

750g / 1 ⅓ lb / 3 cups new or salad
potatoes such as Charlotte or Anya
5 tbsp olive oil
Salt and pepper
½ bunch thyme leaves
2 cloves garlic

- Parboil the potatoes in salted water for 6 minutes or so, until they begin to soften.
- Drain thoroughly, set back over a low heat to drive off any excess moisture.
- Use the end of a rolling pin to lightly crack or crush the potatoes to create crisp edges in the pan.
- Heat the oil in a pan large enough to hold them in one layer, then add the potatoes.
- Season well, toss in the thyme and garlic and sauté until golden and crisp – 10-15 minutes.

167
SERVES 4

Fried Potato Wedges

PREPARATION TIME 15 MINUTES

COOKING TIME 10-15 MINUTES

INGREDIENTS

4 large floury potatoes, scrubbed
5 tbsp olive oil
Salt and pepper
1 tsp paprika (optional)

- Cut the potatoes into wedges lengthways, about 6-8 per potato.
- Parboil in boiling water for 3-4 minutes.
- Drain thoroughly, then set back over a low heat to drive off any excess moisture.
- Heat the oil in a large pan, then add the potatoes and season well.
- Sauté on all sides until golden and crisp.

Fried Potato Wedges with Rosemary and Garlic
168
- Toss with finely chopped rosemary and crushed garlic, then serve with sour cream.

169
SERVES 4

Roast Potato Slices with Béchamel Sauce

PREPARATION TIME 10 MINUTES

COOKING TIME 30 MINUTES

INGREDIENTS

2 large floury potatoes, peeled and cut into thick slices
Salt and pepper
4 tbsp olive oil

FOR THE BÉCHAMEL
1 tbsp butter
1 tbsp plain (all purpose) flour
300ml / 10 fl oz / 1 ¼ cups milk
1 bay leaf
Grated nutmeg
Salt and pepper

- Preheat the oven to 200°C / 400F / gas 7.
- Parboil the potatoes in salted water for 3-4 minutes until starting to soften.
- Drain thoroughly, then tip onto a baking sheet. Toss with olive oil and seasoning and bake in the oven until crisp and golden, turning once – about 20-30 minutes.
- For the béchamel: melt the butter in a pan, stir in the flour to make a paste.
- Whisk in the milk a bit at a time, stirring until the sauce is smooth and thick. Add the bay leaf and leave to cook for 10 minutes, stirring occasionally.
- Season, add the grated nutmeg and remove the bay leaf.
- Pour the sauce over the roasted potato slices.

Roast Potato Slices with Cheese Sauce
170
- Stir 100g / 3 ½ oz gorgonzola into the sauce before serving.

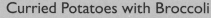

171

SERVES 4

Herby Boiled New Potatoes

- Cook the potatoes in boiling salted water, lid on, for 20 minutes or until tender to the point of a knife.
- Drain thoroughly, then return to the pan.
- Add the butter, seasoning and herbs and swirl to coat the potatoes.
- Serve hot.

PREPARATION TIME 5 MINUTES

COOKING TIME 25 MINUTES

INGREDIENTS

750g / 1 ⅓ lb / 3 cups new potatoes, scrubbed
Salt
50g / 1 ¾ oz butter
Pepper
1 tbsp parsley, chopped
1 tbsp chives, chopped

Boiled New Potatoes with Spiced Butter

172

- Melt the butter with 1 tsp mustard seeds and when popping pour over the potatoes.

173

SERVES 4

Curried Potatoes, Turnips and Spinach

- Cook the potatoes and turnips in boiling salted water for 5 minutes.
- Drain thoroughly.
- Heat the oil in a large lidded pan and cook the mustard seeds for 30 seconds until they pop.
- Add the potatoes and turnips, coat in the spices, add a glass of water and cook with the lid on, turning regularly, for 10 minutes or until golden and starting to crisp.
- Add the spinach and a little more water if the pan looks too dry, put the lid back on and cook until the spinach has wilted.
- Season and serve hot.

PREPARATION TIME 15 MINUTES

COOKING TIME 20 MINUTES

INGREDIENTS

500g / 1 lb / 2 cups floury potatoes, peeled and cut into chunks
1 turnip, peeled and cut into chunks
3 tbsp groundnut oil
1 tsp mustard seeds
½ tbsp ground cumin
½ tbsp ground coriander
1 tsp turmeric
300g / 10 oz / 1 ¼ cups spinach leaves, washed
Salt and pepper

Curried Potatoes with Broccoli

174

- Stir in 1 broccoli head, cut into florets and cooked with the potatoes and omit the spinach.

175

SERVES 6-8 Potato Crisps with Lemon Mustard Dip

Potato Crisps with Herby Sour Cream Dip

176

- Stir chopped dill and mint into a small pot of sour cream.

Potato Crisps with Spicy Mayonnaise

177

- Stir 1-2 tsp harissa or chilli paste into good quality mayonnaise or home made aioli.

Vegetable Crisps

178

- Finely slice parsnips or peeled beetroot and cook in the same way.

PREPARATION TIME 10 MINUTES

COOKING TIME 10 MINUTES

INGREDIENTS

450g / 1 lb/ 2 cups floury potatoes, peeled
1 L / 2 ¼ pints / 4 ¼ cups vegetable oil
Salt or celery salt

FOR THE DIP
50g / 1 ¾ oz / ¼ cup Dijon mustard
1 tbsp grain mustard
1 tbsp crème fraîche
1 tsp honey
Squeeze of lemon juice

- Slice the potatoes into very thin slices either using a mandoline or a very sharp knife – as thin as you can.
- Wash in cold water to get rid of the starch.
- Heat the oil until a cube of bread sizzles immediately when dropped in, then fry the crisps in batches until golden.
- Remove to kitchen paper to drain and sprinkle liberally with salt or a little celery salt.
- To make the dip, mix the ingredients together and serve with the potato crisps.

179
SERVES 4

Roast New Potatoes

- Preheat the oven to 200°C / 400F / gas 7.
- Parboil the potatoes in salted water for 6 minutes until starting to soften.
- Drain thoroughly, then set back over a low heat to drive off any excess moisture.
- Tip into a roasting tin and coat with oil and salt and pepper.
- Roast in the oven for 20-30 minutes until golden and crisp, tossing once.

PREPARATION TIME 10 MINUTES

COOKING TIME 20-30 MINUTES

INGREDIENTS

750g / 1 ⅓ lb/ 3 cups new potatoes, scrubbed
4 tbsp olive oil
Salt and pepper

Roast New Paprika Potatoes
180
- Roll in paprika and ground cumin before baking.

181
SERVES 4

Potatoes with Cumin and Coriander

- Heat the oil in a large pan and add the mustard seeds. Cook for 30 seconds until they start to pop.
- Tip in the potatoes and the spices and a glass of water or vegetable stock, cover with a lid and cook gently for 10-15 minutes until the potatoes are tender. Stir every now and then to prevent sticking.
- To serve, season, sprinkle over the coriander and lemon juice.

PREPARATION TIME 10 MINUTES

COOKING TIME 15 MINUTES

INGREDIENTS

2 tbsp groundnut oil
1 tbsp mustard seeds
500g / 1 lb / 2 cups potatoes, peeled and diced
½ tsp turmeric
½ red chilli, deseeded and finely diced
½ tbsp ground cumin
½ tbsp ground coriander
1 glass water or vegetable stock
½ bunch fresh coriander (cilantro), chopped
Salt and pepper
½ lemon, juiced

Sag Aloo
182
- Stir a small bag of spinach leaves into the potatoes at the end of cooking for an easy take on this Indian classic.

183

SERVES 4

Potato & Red Pepper Cakes

PREPARATION TIME 20 MINUTES

COOKING TIME 15-20 MINUTES

INGREDIENTS

1 tbsp butter
1 red pepper, deseeded and finely diced
1 kg / 2 ¼ lb / 4 ¼ cups cooked potatoes
2 tbsp butter
Salt and pepper
½ bunch parsley or coriander (cilantro), chopped
2 tbsp plain (all purpose) flour, seasoned
Groundnut oil

- Heat the butter in a pan and cook the pepper gently until completely softened.
- Mash the potatoes thoroughly with the butter and salt and pepper until completely smooth. Mix with the peppers and herbs and shape into patties.
- Dust both sides with seasoned flour.
- Heat a thin film of oil in a pan and cook the potato cakes 2 at a time until golden and crisp on both sides.

Potato Mixed Pepper Cakes   184

- Use a mixture of ½ yellow, ½ red for colour.

185

SERVES 4

Oven-Baked Wedges

PREPARATION TIME 15 MINUTES

COOKING TIME 30 MINUTES

INGREDIENTS

4 large floury potatoes, scrubbed
5 tbsp olive oil
Salt
1 tsp paprika
Pinch Cayenne pepper
½ tsp celery salt
1 tsp dried oregano
Tomato relish or chutney, to serve

- Preheat the oven to 220°C / 450F / gas 7.
- Cut the potatoes into wedges lengthways, about 6-8 per potato. Parboil in salted water for 3-4 minutes.
- Drain thoroughly, then set back over a low heat to drive off any excess moisture.
- Place on a baking sheet and toss with the oil and seasonings until thoroughly coated.
- Bake in the oven for about 30 minutes until deep gold and crisp.
- Drain briefly on kitchen paper and serve with chutney or relish for dipping.

Wedges with Crispy Bacon Shards   186

- Grill streaky bacon until very crisp and blitz in a food processor to crumbs. Scatter over the potato wedges.

SERVES 4 Potato Salad

187

Potato Salad with Dill Mayonnaise
188

- Stir chopped dill through the mayo rather than parsley.

Potato Salad with Horseradish
189

- Stir 1 tbsp creamed horseradish into the mayonnaise for a fiery version.

Potato Salad with Capers
190

- Add 2 tbsp capers to the mayonnaise.

PREPARATION TIME 5 MINUTES

COOKING TIME 20 MINUTES

INGREDIENTS

1 kg / 2 ¼ lb / 4 ¼ cups new or salad potatoes such as Anya or Charlotte
2 sprigs mint
Salt
200g / 7 oz / ¾ cup mayonnaise
½ bunch chives, chopped
2 spring onions (scallions), chopped
½ bunch parsley, chopped
Salt and pepper

- Cook the potatoes whole in boiling salted water with the mint sprigs, covered with a lid, for about 20 minutes or until tender.
- Drain thoroughly.
- Leave to cool slightly then slice thickly.
- Mix the mayonnaise with the herbs and seasoning and toss with the potatoes while still warm.

VEGETABLES

SERVES 4

Vegetable Cous Cous

- Place the cous cous in a bowl, cover with the hot stock and clingfilm the bowl. Leave for 10 minutes or so until tender, then fork through the grains and add the lemon.
- Meanwhile heat the oil in a pan and sauté the garlic, carrots and diced peppers and toss to coat and cook for 3 minutes.
- Add the beans and cover with vegetable stock and leave to simmer for 5-8 minutes until all is tender.
- Add the tomatoes and heat through.
- Tip the sautéed vegetables into the cous cous.
- Season generously then add the parsley and pine nuts and serve.

PREPARATION TIME 15 MINUTES

COOKING TIME 12 MINUTES

INGREDIENTS

250g / 9 oz / 1 cup cous cous
2 tbsp sultanas
250ml / 9 fl oz / 1 cup stock
Squeeze of lemon juice
2 tbsp olive oil
1 clove garlic, crushed
2 carrots, peeled and thickly sliced
1 red pepper, finely chopped
1 yellow pepper, finely chopped
Handful green beans
150ml / 5 fl oz / ⅔ cup vegetable stock
4 tomatoes, chopped
Salt and pepper
½ bunch parsley, roughly chopped
2 tbsp pine nuts, toasted

Cauliflower Gratin

SERVES 4-6

PREPARATION TIME 20 MINUTES

COOKING TIME 20 MINUTES

INGREDIENTS

1 head cauliflower
100g / 3 ½ oz / ½ cup butter
2 tbsp plain (all purpose) flour
1 tsp mustard powder

2 bay leaves
Grated nutmeg
¼ tsp mace
500ml / 1 pint / 2 cups milk
275g / 10 oz / 1 ¼ cups Cheddar, grated

- Cut the cauliflower into florets and cook in boiling salted water for 5 minutes. Drain well and set aside.
- Preheat the oven to 200°C / 400F / gas 6.
- Heat the butter in a pan and whisk in the flour and mustard powder to make a paste. Gradually whisk in the milk and stir until thick and smooth. Add the bay leaves, nutmeg and mace and leave to simmer gently, stirring occasionally, for 10 minutes.
- Stir in most of the cheese until melted.
- Tip the cauliflower into a baking dish and spoon over the sauce. sprinkle with the remaining cheese and bake for 20 minutes.

Chestnut and Bacon Srouts

SERVES 4

PREPARATION TIME 5 MINUTES

COOKING TIME 10 MINUTES

INGREDIENTS

400g / 14 oz / 1 ½ cups Brussels sprouts
30g / 1 oz butter
250g / 9 oz / 1 cup smoked streaky

bacon, chopped
400g / 14 oz / 1 ½ cups vacuum-packed peeled chestnuts
100ml / 3 ½ fl oz / ½ cup dry white wine
Salt and pepper

- Remove any tough outer leaves from the sprouts.
- Bring a pan of salted water to the boil and cook the sprouts until just tender – 3-4 minutes.
- Drain and set aside to cool. Cut the sprouts in half.
- Heat the butter in a pan and add the bacon, frying until crisp and golden.
- Remove the bacon with a slotted spoon, then add the halved sprouts and chestnuts and the wine.
- Cook at a fast simmer until the wine has reduced to a syrupy consistency, then return the bacon to the pan and adjust the seasoning.

194

SERVES 4

Aubergine alla Parmigiana

PREPARATION TIME 30 MINUTES

COOKING TIME 20 MINUTES

....

INGREDIENTS

6 tbsp olive oil
1 tbsp dried oregano
3 aubergines (eggplants), thinly
sliced lengthways
1 onion, peeled and chopped
2 cloves garlic, finely sliced
1 cinnamon stick
2 x 400g can chopped tomatoes
1 bunch basil
2 balls mozzarella
60g / 2 oz / ¼ cup Parmesan, grated

- Preheat the oven to 200°C / 400F / gas 6.
- Pour the oil and oregano onto a baking sheet and 'smoosh' the aubergine slices around in it on both sides. Bake for 15 minutes or until tender and golden. Drain on kitchen paper.
- Meanwhile heat a little oil in a pan and gently fry the onion and garlic until completely soft.
- Add the cinnamon stick and basil stalks, add the tomatoes and simmer for 20 minutes, season.
- Spoon a little sauce into the bottom of a gratin dish then layer aubergines, sauce and mozzarella to the top of the dish, seasoning as you go, finishing with a layer of sauce.
- Sprinkle over the Parmesan and bake for 15-20 minutes until golden and bubbling.

Aubergine Parmigiana   195
with Courgettes

- Add 2 thinly sliced courgettes, layering them with the aubergines, for a summer version.

196

SERVES 4

Confit Carrots

PREPARATION TIME 5 MINUTES

COOKING TIME 2 HOURS

....

INGREDIENTS

350g / 12 oz / 1 ½ cups Chantenay
or baby carrots, scrubbed
250g / 9 oz / 1 cup melted duck fat
2 cloves garlic, finely sliced
4 sprigs thyme

- Preheat oven to 140°C / 275F / gas 1.
- Lay the carrots in a baking dish and cover with duck fat, garlic and thyme, adding more fat if necessary to completely submerge the carrots.
- Bake in the oven for 2 hours until completely tender.
- Remove from the fat. For a crisp brown exterior, fry them off in a pan before serving.

Confit Carrots with Orange   197

- A strip of orange peel in the duck fat – no pith – will add to the French feel.

198

SERVES 4 # Mushy Peas

- Heat the olive oil gently in a pan and add the peas and spring onions. Cook until they turn bright vivid green, then add the mint, seasoning and a little sugar.
- Crush with a potato masher and add the butter.
- Serve hot.

PREPARATION TIME 5 MINUTES

COOKING TIME 10 MINUTES

INGREDIENTS

4 tbsp olive oil
500g / 1 lb / 2 cups frozen peas
3 spring onions, (scallions), finely chopped
1 bunch mint leaves, chopped
Salt and pepper
1 tsp sugar
30g / 1 oz butter

Mashed Broad Beans   199

- Use double podded broad beans in the same way.

200

SERVES 4 # Roasted Rosemary Tomatoes

- Preheat the oven to 150C/310F/Gas 2.
- Place the tomato halves in a single layer in a baking dish and drizzle generously with oil. Season and tuck the rosemary in between the tomatoes.
- Bake for 2-3 hours or even longer until the tomatoes have collapsed but retain their shape.

PREPARATION TIME 5 MINUTES

COOKING TIME 2-3 HOURS

INGREDIENTS

500g / 1 lb / 2 cups ripe tomatoes, halved
4 tbsp olive oil
2 branches rosemary
Salt and pepper

Roasted Tomatoes with   201
Sherry Vinegar

- Sprinkle with 1 tbsp sherry vinegar before roasting.

202

SERVES 4

Grilled Red Peppers

PREPARATION TIME 5 MINUTES

COOKING TIME 40-50 MINUTES

INGREDIENTS

4 red peppers
Olive oil
Salt and pepper

- Preheat the oven to 200°C / 400F / gas 6.
- Halve and deseed the peppers and place in a roasting tin.
- Drizzle with oil and season and roast in the oven for at least 40 minutes until blackened and collapsed.
- To remove the skins, place in a freezer bag and leave to steam for 10 minutes before removing the skins.

Grilled Mixed Peppers 203

- You can grill yellow and orange peppers the same way. Store under olive oil in the fridge.

204

SERVES 4

Italian-style Courgettes

PREPARATION TIME 15 MINUTES

COOKING TIME 20 MINUTES

INGREDIENTS

4 courgettes (zucchini)
200g / 6 ½ oz / ¾ cup ricotta
1 tbsp parsley, finely chopped
1 tbsp basil, finely chopped
1 tbsp mint, finely chopped
Salt and pepper
Extra virgin olive oil
4 tbsp Parmesan, grated

- Preheat the oven to 200°C / 400F / gas 6.
- Slice the courgettes in half lengthways and scoop out the flesh, leaving the sides intact.
- Finely dice the flesh. Heat 2 tbsp oil in a pan and cook the courgette flesh until tender. Tip into a bowl and leave to cool.
- Once cool, stir into the ricotta, herbs and season well.
- Use a spoon to stuff the interiors of the courgettes, drizzle with oil and sprinkle over the Parmesan.
- Bake in the oven for about 20 minutes or until the courgettes are tender and bubbling.

Italian Style Courgettes with Ricotta and Anchovies 205

- Add 4 chopped anchovies to the oil and cook until 'melted', then add the courgette flesh and proceed as

206

SERVES 4

Ratatouille

Crisp Ratatouille 207

- Cook the vegetables for less time so they remain crisp tender for a different salad-style texture.

Asian Style Ratatouille 208

- Omit the coriander seeds and basil and use finely chopped ginger and a touch of 5 spice.

Ratatouille with Risotto 209

- Stir into rice or risotto for a filling vegetarian supper.

PREPARATION TIME 10 MINUTES

COOKING TIME 50 MINUTES

INGREDIENTS

4-6 tbsp olive oil
2 onions, peeled and finely sliced
2 aubergines (eggplants), cut in half lengthways and finely sliced
3 courgettes (zucchini), cut in half lengthways and finely sliced
2 cloves garlic, finely chopped
3 red peppers, seeded and cut into strips
1 x 400g can chopped tomatoes
1 tsp coriander seeds, crushed
Salt and pepper
Handful fresh basil leaves

- Heat the oil in a pan and cook the onions until deep gold and sweet.
- Add the aubergines and cook for 2 minutes, then add the courgettes and garlic and cook for 2 minutes, then add the peppers and cook for 5 minutes.
- Add the tomatoes and coriander seeds and leave to simmer for at least 30 minutes over a very low heat, stirring occasionally, until the vegetables are very soft.
- Season and sprinkle over the basil before serving.

210

SERVES 4

Provencal Stuffed Tomatoes

Bacon Stuffed Tomatoes   211

- Stir in 2 rashers of bacon, finely chopped and fried, into the mixture.

Tuna Stuffed Tomatoes   212

- Omit the rosemary, but stir canned tuna into the mixture.

Taleggio Stuffed Tomatoes   213

- Stir cubes of taleggio into the breadcrumbs and bake until oozing.

PREPARATION TIME 40 MINUTES

COOKING TIME 30 MINUTES

....

INGREDIENTS

8 ripe beef tomatoes
Salt
1 tbsp olive oil
1 onion, peeled and finely chopped
2 cloves garlic, finely chopped
300g / 10 oz / 1 ¼ cups breadcrumbs
1 tbsp rosemary leaves, finely chopped
½ bunch parsley, finely chopped
2 tbsp Parmesan, grated

- Using a teaspoon, hollow out the tomatoes, discarding the seeds.
- Sprinkle the insides with a little salt and leave to drain upside down for 30 minutes.
- Meanwhile fry the onion and garlic in the oil until translucent.
- Add the breadcrumbs, rosemary and parsley and season.
- Stir in the Parmesan and leave to cool a little.
- Preheat the oven to 200°C / 400F / gas 6.
- Fill the tomatoes with the mixture and place in a roasting tin.
- Drizzle with olive oil and bake in the oven for about 30 minutes or until the tomatoes are soft but retaining their shape.

214

SERVES 4

Vegetable & Bean Estouffade

- Heat the butter in a shallow pan and gently cook the onions without colouring.
- Add the carrots and leeks and cook until softened.
- Add the mushrooms and cannellini beans, then pour in the stock.
- Add the dulse and thyme and simmer very gently until the liquid has nearly evaporated and the vegetables are very tender.
- Season and serve.

PREPARATION TIME 15 MINUTES

COOKING TIME 30 MINUTES

....

INGREDIENTS

30g / 1 oz butter
1 onion, peeled and finely sliced
2 carrots, peeled and finely sliced
2 leeks, white part only, finely sliced
200g / 7 oz / ¾ cup button mushrooms, sliced
2 x 400g can cannellini beans, drained
200ml / 7 fl oz / ¾ cup vegetable stock
2 tbsp dulse (sea lettuce), finely chopped
2 sprigs thyme
Salt and pepper

Vegetable Estouffade with Butter Beans

215

- Try using meatier butter beans instead of cannellini.

216

SERVES 4

Pan-fried Carrots and Parsnips

- Cut the carrots and parsnips lengthways into thin slices.
- Parboil the vegetables for 2 minutes to soften, then drain and dry thoroughly.
- Heat the oil in a pan and fry the carrot and parsnip slices in batches until crisp and browned with the thyme.
- At the end of cooking toss with the vinegar and season well.

PREPARATION TIME 10 MINUTES

COOKING TIME 20 MINUTES

....

INGREDIENTS

4 large carrots, peeled
2 parsnips, peeled
4 tbsp olive oil
4 sprigs thyme
1 tbsp red wine vinegar
Salt and pepper

Carrots and Parsnips with Balsamic Vinegar

217

- For a sweeter note, use balsamic in place of the red wine vinegar.

SALADS

218
SERVES 4

Crunchy Asian Salad

- Peel the carrots and cut into matchsticks. Place in a bowl.
- Thinly slice the radishes and add to the carrots.
- Add the pepper, beans and cabbage.
- Whisk together the salt, vinegar and sugar and pour over the vegetables, coating thoroughly. Leave for 20 minutes, then serve.

PREPARATION TIME 30 MINUTES

INGREDIENTS

2 carrots
1 bunch radishes, washed
2 green peppers, deseeded and finely sliced
Handful green beans, lightly cooked
1/8 white cabbage, cored and finely shredded
1 tsp salt
5 tbsp rice vinegar
6 tbsp sugar

Fennel, Radish & Orange Salad

219
SERVES 4

PREPARATION TIME 10 MINUTES

INGREDIENTS

1 fennel (finocchio) bulb
1 orange
½ bunch radishes
1 tbsp red wine vinegar
4 tbsp extra virgin olive oil
Salt and pepper

- Halve and core the fennel bulb, remove the outer leaves. Slice very finely and tip into a bowl.
- Peel the orange and remove any pith. Holding it over the fennel bowl, cut out the orange segments and add to the fennel.
- Finely slice the radishes.
- Whisk together the vinegar and oil with a little seasoning, toss thoroughly with the salad and serve.

Tomato Salad

220
SERVES 4

PREPARATION TIME 20 MINUTES

INGREDIENTS

500g / 1 lb / 2 cups mixed heritage tomatoes
½ clove garlic, crushed
1 tbsp red wine or balsamic vinegar
6 tbsp extra virgin olive oil
½ red onion, finely sliced
4 radishes, thinly sliced
½ bunch basil
Salt and pepper

- Roughly chop the tomatoes any which way and tip into a bowl.
- Sprinkle over a little salt and leave for 10 minutes.
- Whisk together the garlic, vinegar and oil until thickened.
- Add the onion and radishes to the tomatoes, tip in the dressing and toss thoroughly to coat.
- Decorate with torn basil leaves and serve.

Salad Niçoise

221

SERVES 4

Salad Niçoise with Canned Tuna

222

- Traditionally this salad was made with canned tuna, so feel free to use as a more economical substitute.

Salad Niçoise with Anchovies

223

- Fresh anchovies add punch to this salad.

Salad Niçoise with Chicken

224

- Hot or cold chicken would add substance to the salad.

PREPARATION TIME 30 MINUTES

COOKING TIME 10 MINUTES

....

4 eggs at room temperature
120g / 4 oz / ½ cup fine green beans, topped and tailed
4 tuna steaks, 2.5cm thick
8-10 small new potatoes, cooked whole and quartered
8 plum tomatoes, quartered
4 Little Gem lettuces, quartered lengthways
8 anchovy fillets
Handful black olives
½ bunch parsley, roughly chopped

FOR THE DRESSING
3 tbsp red wine vinegar
½ clove garlic, crushed
Salt and pepper
100ml / 3/12 fl oz / ½ cup extra virgin olive oil

- Whisk together the red wine vinegar and garlic, season and whisk in the oil until emulsified. Set aside.
- Cook the eggs for 5 minutes in boiling water, then cool and remove the shells.
- Cook the green beans in boiling salted water for 4 minutes, then drain and plunge into iced water. Set aside.
- Heat a griddle and cook the tuna steaks, oiled and seasoned, on each side for 90 seconds, then set aside to rest.
- On a large platter, arrange the lettuce leaves and cooked potatoes. Cut the eggs in half and arrange amongst the leaves. Slice the tuna thickly and add to the plate with the tomatoes, anchovies and olives.
- Drizzle with dressing and scatter with parsley before serving.

225

SERVES 4

Chinese Cabbage and Apple Salad

- Halve the cabbage, remove the core and very finely shred the leaves.
- Core the apple and cut into thin matchsticks.
- Deseed and finely slice the pepper. Place the salad ingredients in a bowl.
- Whisk together the soy, ginger and lime. Whisk in the oils until emulsified.
- Toss the salad in the dressing and leave for 10 minutes to soften slightly.
- Serve on a platter, decorated with coriander and sprinkle with black sesame seeds.

PREPARATION TIME 15 MINUTES

INGREDIENTS

1 Chinese cabbage
2 eating apples
1 red pepper
1 bunch coriander (cilantro), finely chopped
2 tbsp black sesame seeds

FOR THE DRESSING
2 tbsp soy sauce
1 tsp fresh ginger, grated
½ lime, juiced
1 tsp sesame oil
1 tbsp groundnut oil

White Cabbage and Apple Salad   226

- If you can't source Chinese cabbage, very finely shredded white cabbage would do.

227

SERVES 4

Smoked Salmon and Spinach Salad

- Cook the mange tout for 2 minutes in boiling salted water then drain and plunge into iced water.
- Arrange the salad leaves on a large platter and decorate with smoked salmon and mange tout.
- Toast the walnuts lightly under a hot grill for a few seconds, then add to the platter.
- Whisk together the dressing until emulsified, then drizzle over the salad. Decorate with the flowers and serve.

PREPARATION TIME 10 MINUTES

COOKING TIME 2 MINUTES

INGREDIENTS

100g / 3 ½ oz / ½ cup mange tout (snow peas)
120g / 4 oz / ½ cup baby spinach leaves
100g / 3 ½ oz / ½ cup mache (corn lettuce)
200g / 7 oz / ¾ cup smoked salmon slices
50g / 1 ¾ oz / ¼ cup walnuts
Handful edible flowers, washed

FOR THE DRESSING
2 tbsp lemon juice
½ red chilli, deseeded and very finely chopped
6 tbsp extra virgin olive oil
Salt and pepper

Fresh Salmon Spinach Salad   228

- Fresh salmon fillets would work well with these ingredients whilst giving a milder flavour.

229
SERVES 4

Prawns, Mushrooms and Caper Salad

PREPARATION TIME 10 MINUTES

COOKING TIME 10 MINUTES

INGREDIENTS

320g / 11 oz / 1 ½ cups fusilli pasta
200g / 7 oz / ¾ cup cooked king prawns (shrimp)
100g / 3 ½ oz / ½ cup button mushrooms
2 tbsp capers, drained
8 cherry tomatoes
1-2 tbsp red wine vinegar
6 tbsp extra virgin olive oil
Salt and pepper

- Cook the pasta in boiling salted water according to packet instructions.
- Drain and tip into a bowl.
- Add the prawns. Finely slice the mushrooms and add with the capers.
- Halve the tomatoes and add to the pasta.
- Whisk together the vinegar and oil and toss the salad in the dressing. Season and serve.

Pasta Salad with Basil Dressing 230
- Peppery basil complements all the ingredients. Try whizzing a handful of leaves in a little oil and trickling over.

231
SERVES 4

Apple & Goats' Cheese Salad

PREPARATION TIME 15 MINUTES

INGREDIENTS

2 crisp green eating apples
Lemon juice
200g / 7 oz / ¾ cup log goats' cheese
100g / 3 ½ oz / ½ cup button mushrooms
½ pomegranate
1 small romaine lettuce, cut into ribbons

- Halve the apples and core, then slice into thin half moons. Tip into a bowl and stir in a little lemon juice to prevent browning.
- Cut the cheese into thick slices and arrange on a plate with the apple slices and lettuce ribbons.
- Finely slice the mushrooms and scatter around the cheese.
- Holding the pomegranate half skin side up, bash with a wooden spoon to release the seeds.

Apple & Goats' Cheese Salad with a Honey Mustard Dressing 232
- Whisk 1 tbsp wholegrain mustard with ½ tbsp honey, a little seasoning and extra virgin oil then drizzle over for extra tang.

Pasta, Ham and Artichoke Salad

233

SERVES 4

- Cook the pasta in boiling salted water until al dente. Drain thoroughly, then toss with a little olive oil and leave to cool.
- Mix together the artichokes, chopped ham, tomatoes and rocket in a bowl.
- For the dressing: whisk together the vinegar, mustard, salt, pepper and sugar. Whisk in the oil until thickened and amalgamated. Check the seasoning and adjust if necessary.
- Add the pasta to the other ingredients, pour over the dressing then, using large spoons, toss everything until coated.

PREPARATION TIME 20 MINUTES

COOKING TIME 10 MINUTES

INGREDIENTS

300g / 10 oz / 1 ¼ cups pasta
1 jar artichoke hearts, drained
200g / 7 oz / ¾ cup ham, trimmed and cut into cubes
300g / 10 oz / 1 ¼ cups cherry tomatoes, halved
60g rocket (arugula) leaves

FOR THE DRESSING
2-3 tsp red wine vinegar
½ - 1 tsp grain mustard
½ tsp salt
Pepper
Pinch sugar
6 tbsp extra virgin olive oil

Pasta Prawn Artichoke Salad   234

- Try adding cooked prawns instead of ham if you want a lighter option.

Chicken, Grape and Walnut Salad

235

SERVES 4

- Preheat the oven to 200°C / 400F / gas 6.
- Roast the chicken breasts, drizzled with oil and a little lemon juice and seasoned for 25 minutes, until just cooked through. Leave to rest.
- Toss the grapes, walnuts and lettuce leaves together.
- Grate the carrot and toss with the salad.
- Thickly slice the chicken, removing the skin if desired and add to the leaves.
- Squeeze a little more lemon juice and the extra virgin olive oil into the roasting tin and whisk in. Spoon the juices over the salad sparingly and serve.

PREPARATION TIME 10 MINUTES

COOKING TIME 25 MINUTES

INGREDIENTS

4 chicken breasts, skin on
Olive oil
Salt and pepper
Juice of ½ lemon
80g / 2 ½ oz / ⅓ cup green grapes
80g / 2 ½ oz / ⅓ cup walnuts
3 Little Gem lettuces
1 carrot, peeled
2 tbsp extra virgin olive oil

Chicken, Grape and Walnut Salad with a Creamy Dressing   236

- Mix 4-5 tbsp crème fraîche with a little lemon juice and 1 tbsp wholegrain mustard for a creamy dressing.

BEEF

Home-Made Burgers

- Season the meat well, mix well with the mustard if using and form into patties around 2 cm thick. Refrigerate until needed.
- Heat a griddle to very hot, then brush the burgers on each side with a little oil. Cook for 3-4 minutes each side, then leave to rest for 5-8 minutes wrapped in foil, the slices of cheese melting on top. Serve in buns topped with tomatoes, red onion and salad.

PREPARATION TIME 10 MINUTES

COOKING TIME 25 MINUTES

INGREDIENTS

4 sirloin steaks, minced until coarsely ground but not mush (ask your butcher)
1 tsp salt
1 tbsp grain mustard (optional)
Black pepper
Olive oil
4 slices Jarlsberg cheese
1 large tomato, thickly sliced
4 burger buns

Beef Meatballs in Tomato Sauce

PREPARATION TIME 20 MINUTES
+ CHILLING TIME

COOKING TIME 30 MINUTES

INGREDIENTS

400g / 14 oz / 1 ½ cups minced beef
1 egg
2 tbsp parsley, chopped

1 clove garlic, crushed
½ lemon, grated zest
Salt and pepper
1 thick slice of white bread, crusts removed soaked in 2 tbsp milk
3 tbsp olive oil
1 x 400g can chopped tomatoes
400ml / 14 fl oz / 1 ½ cups beef stock
1 tsp sugar

- Place the meat in a large bowl with the egg, garlic, lemon zest and 1 tbsp parsley and season.
- Mulch the bread in your fingers and crumble into the mix. Mix everything together with your hands to become smooth and sticky.
- Roll into small walnut-sized balls with cold wet hands, place on a tray and chill for 30 minutes.
- Heat the oil in a pan and fry the meatballs in batches until brown.
- Add the tomatoes and stock, then add the sugar and season and bring to the boil. Lower the heat and simmer for about 20 minutes.
- Serve with pasta or cous cous.

Beef Wellington

PREPARATION TIME 45 MINUTES

COOKING TIME 20 MINUTES

INGREDIENTS

1 beef fillet, weighing 1 kg / 2 ¼ lb
3 tbsp olive oil
3 tbsp butter
250g / 9 oz / 1 cup mushrooms

1 shallot, finely chopped
2 sprigs thyme leaves
75ml / 2 ½ oz / ⅓ cup dry white wine
1 sheet ready rolled puff pastry
1 tbsp flour
2 egg yolks, beaten

TO SERVE

750g / 1 ⅓ lb / 3 cups new potatoes, roasted

- Preheat oven to 220°C (200° fan)/ 450F / gas 7.
- Place the beef in a roasting tin, drizzle with oil and roast for 15 minutes.
- Meanwhile, place the mushrooms in a food processor with the shallot and process as finely as possible.
- Heat the butter in a pan and dry the mushroom mixture with thyme leaves and a little seasoning until softened. Add the wine and cook until the wine has been absorbed. Set aside to cool.
- Roll the pastry out a little more on a floured surface. Spoon the cooled mushrooms over the pastry, leaving a small margin around the edges.
- Place the beef in the centre and roll the pastry up like sausage, fully encasing the beef. Seal the edges with egg yolk, then brush the pastry with the remaining egg.
- Reduce the oven to 200°C (180° fan)/ 400F / gas 6 and roast for 20 minutes until puffed and golden.

240

SERVES 4

Burritos

PREPARATION TIME 25 MINUTES

COOKING TIME 10 MINUTES

INGREDIENTS

2 tbsp vegetable oil
1 onion, peeled and finely sliced
350g / 12 oz / 1 ½ cups rump steak, finely sliced
1 clove garlic, finely chopped
½ green chilli, finely chopped
1 tsp paprika
1 tbsp Worcestershire sauce
Salt and pepper

TO SERVE

4 flour tortillas, warmed briefly
400g / 14 oz / 1 ½ cups refried beans, heated through
100g / 3 ½ oz / ½ cup Cheddar, grated
Guacamole
Tomato salsa
Sour cream

- Heat the oil in a pan and fry the onion until softened.
- Add the steak, increase the heat and fry quickly for 2 minutes, adding the garlic, chilli, paprika and Worcestershire sauce. Remove from the heat.
- Lay the tortillas out on a surface and spoon the steak mixture down the middle and top with a line of refried beans.
- Wrap the tortilla around the filling and place on a baking sheet, seam side down. Scatter with cheddar.
- Grill until cheese has melted and serve with accompanying sauces.

Chicken or Lamb Burritos

241

- Try the burritos made with pinkly-cooked lamb or chicken strips.

242

SERVES 4

Chilli con Carne

PREPARATION TIME 20 MINUTES

COOKING TIME 2 HOURS 10 MINUTES

INGREDIENTS

2 tbsp vegetable oil
500g / 1 lb / 2 full cups stewing beef, diced
1 onion, peeled and chopped
2 cloves garlic, finely chopped
1 tsp paprika
1 tsp ground cumin
1 tsp cinnamon
½ - 1 tsp Cayenne pepper or ½ tsp dried chilli flakes
1 x 400g can kidney beans
1 x 400g can chopped tomatoes
300ml / 10 fl oz / 1 ¼ cups beef stock
20g / ½ oz dark chocolate, finely chopped

TO SERVE

1 lime, juiced
Sour cream
Rice

- Heat the oil in a large casserole and cook the beef until browned. Remove with a slotted spoon.
- Add the onion and garlic and fry for a further 5 minutes until golden.
- Add the spices and mix well, then pour over the kidney beans, tomatoes and stock, add the beef back in and bring to the boil.
- Simmer over a low heat for at least 2 hours, stirring occasionally, until the chilli has thickened and reduced.
- When the meat is falling apart, stir in the chocolate and season.
- Serve with a squeeze of lime juice, sour cream and rice.

Baked Chilli with Crispy Crust

243

- Tip the chilli into a gratin dish, top with lightly crushed tortilla chips and blue cheese and bake for 20 minutes.

244 | SERVES 4-6 — Cottage Pie

- Preheat the oven to 180°C (160° fan) / 350F / gas 4.
- Heat the oil in a large pan and briskly fry the lamb mince. Add the vegetables and sweat until soft.
- Stir in the tomato puree and cook out for 2 minutes, before adding the herbs and pouring over the stock. Simmer until the stock has reduced and there is just a little liquid left in the bottom of the pan.
- Meanwhile cook the potatoes in boiling salted water until tender to the point of a knife.
- Drain thoroughly, then mash until completely smooth with the butter and season well.
- Pour the lamb base into a baking dish, then spoon over the mashed potato. Run a fork down the length of the potato to create edges that will crisp in the oven.
- Bake for 30 minutes until bubbling and golden.

Cottage Pie with Horseradish Potato Crust — 245

- Stir 1-2 tbsp creamed horseradish into the mashed potatoes before spooning over.

PREPARATION TIME 25 MINUTES

COOKING TIME 35 MINUTES

INGREDIENTS

2 tbsp vegetable oil
450g / 1 lb / 2 cups minced beef
1 onion, peeled and finely chopped
2 carrots, peeled and finely chopped
2 sticks celery, finely chopped
100g / 3 ½ oz / ½ cup flat field mushrooms, finely chopped
1 tbsp tomato puree
1 bay leaf
1 sprig rosemary
350ml / 12 fl oz / 1 ½ cups beef stock
Salt and pepper

900g / 2 lb / 3 ½ cups floury potatoes, peeled and cut into chunks
100g / 3 ½ oz / ½ cup butter

246 | SERVES 6 — Beef Stew

- Heat the oil in a casserole. Dust the beef with flour and sear in the oil on all sides, in batches, removing as you go with a slotted spoon.
- Cook the carrots, onions and celery until softened, then stir in the tomato puree.
- Add the beef back to the pan with any resting juices and the bouquet garni, then pour in the red wine and stock and bring to a simmer.
- Reduce the heat, season, partially cover with a lid and cook very gently for 2-3 hours until the meat is tender.
- Serve with mashed potato.

Beef Stew with Port and Mustard — 247

- Use port instead of the red wine for a sweeter flavour and balance with a good tbsp Dijon or wholegrain mustard.

PREPARATION TIME 45 MINUTES

COOKING TIME 3 ½ HOURS

INGREDIENTS

3 tbsp vegetable oil
600g / 1 ⅓ lb / 2 ½ cups stewing beef, cubed
1 tbsp seasoned flour
2 carrots, peeled and cut into short lengths
2 onions, peeled and sliced
2 sticks celery, finely chopped
1 tbsp tomato puree
1 bouquet garni
300ml / 10 fl oz / 1 ¼ cups red wine
500ml / 1 pint / 2 cups beef stock
Salt and pepper

248

SERVES 6

Beef Bourguignon

PREPARATION TIME 15 MINUTES

COOKING TIME 3 HOURS

INGREDIENTS

1 kg / 2 ¼ lb / 4 ¼ cups stewing beef, cubed
225 g / 7 ½ oz / 1 ½ cups baby carrots, washed and scrubbed
3 tbsp vegetable oil
1 onion, peeled and sliced
1 tbsp flour
400ml / 14 fl oz / 1 ½ cups red wine, preferably Burgundy
2 cloves garlic, sliced
1 sprig thyme
1 bay leaf
12 pearl or button onions, peeled
225g / 8 oz / 1 cup smoked streaky bacon, diced
200g / 7 oz / ¾ cup chestnut mushrooms
Salt and pepper

- Preheat the oven to 140°C / 275F / gas 1.
- Sear the beef in 1 tbsp oil in a casserole until brown all over. Remove with a slotted spoon.
- Add the onion and cook until beginning to brown, then return the meat to the pan.
- Stir in the flour and soak up the juices, then pour in the wine. Add the garlic and herbs, season, cover with a lid and cook for 2 hours.
- Meanwhile fry the onions and bacon in a little oil, then add, with the mushrooms and carrots to the casserole and cook for 1 more hour.
- Adjust the seasoning and serve.

Beef Bourguignon with Garlic Bread

249

- For the last 20 minutes of cooking, top with thin slices of toasted baguette spread with garlic butter.

250

SERVES 6

Thai Beef Green Curry

PREPARATION TIME 15 MINUTES

COOKING TIME 45 MINUTES

INGREDIENTS

500ml / 1 pint / 2 cups coconut milk
750g / 1 ⅓ lb / 3 cups rump steak, sliced
2 aubergines (eggplant), chopped
1-2 tbsp caster (superfine) sugar
1-2 tbsp fish sauce
2 limes, juiced
Thai basil

FOR THE CURRY PASTE

1 tbsp coriander seeds
1 tbsp cumin seeds
½ - 1 tbsp black peppercorns
2-4 green chillies
8 cloves garlic, peeled
2 stalks lemongrass
1 bunch coriander (cilantro)
2 tbsp fresh galangal or ginger
3 kaffir lime leaves
6 shallots, peeled
1 tbsp dried shrimp paste

- Pound the seeds in a pestle and mortar or in a freezer bag with a rolling pin until finely ground.
- Tip into a food processor and whiz with the rest of the ingredients until smooth. You will only need 4-5 tbsp for this recipe, so keep the rest in a sealed jar in the fridge.
- Heat a wok and add 4-5 tbsp curry paste and 2 tbsp of the cream off the top of the coconut milk and stir until sizzling.
- Add the beef and coat thoroughly in the paste, then pour in the coconut milk.
- Add the aubergines, sugar, fish sauce and juice of 1 lime and simmer gently for about 15-20 minutes or until the aubergine is cooked and tender.
- Adjust the flavours with more sugar, fish sauce and lime juice, then serve with Thai sticky rice, sprinkled with coriander and Thai basil leaves.

Thai Seafood Green Curry

251

- Make it with mixed seafood such as prawns, squid and chunky white fish.

Fried Chilli Beef with Noodles

252

SERVES 2

- Whisk together the eggs, salt and cornflour and coat the beef strips.
- Heat the oil to 180°C / 350F and deep fry the beef in small batches. Cook for about 5 minutes until brown and crisp. Remove and drain on kitchen paper.
- Heat a little oil in a wok and stir fry the carrots, spring onion and chilli. Add the remaining ingredients and toss together, adding the beef at the last minute.
- Cook the noodles according to packet instructions and serve topped with the chilli beef.

PREPARATION TIME 10 MINUTES

COOKING TIME 15 MINUTES

INGREDIENTS

2 eggs, beaten
½ tsp salt
1 ½ tbsp cornflour (cornstarch)
150g / 5 oz / ⅔ cup rump steak, sliced
Vegetable oil for deep frying
1 carrot, shredded
2 spring onions (scallions), chopped
1 red chilli, deseeded chopped
1 tsp sugar
2 tbsp rice vinegar
2 tbsp sweet chilli sauce
1 tbsp soy sauce
Noodles, to accompany

253

SERVES 4

Beef Stroganoff

PREPARATION TIME 15 MINUTES

COOKING TIME 20 MINUTES

INGREDIENTS

2 tbsp butter
1 onion, peeled and sliced
2 cloves garlic, finely sliced
400g / 14 oz / 1 ½ cups mushrooms, sliced

500g / 1 lb/ 2 cups sirloin or rump steak, thinly sliced
Salt and pepper
275ml / 10 fl oz / 1 cup sour cream
1 tbsp smoked paprika

TO GARNISH

Chopped cornichons
Flat leaf parsley
Boiled rice

- Fry the onions and garlic in the butter until golden and sweet then add the mushrooms. Cook until all the liquid has evaporated and season. Remove from the pan with a slotted spoon.
- Increase the heat and fry the beef quickly for 2 minutes, then return the vegetables to the pan and pour in the sour cream and paprika.
- Bubble up, adjust the seasoning and serve with the garnishes.

254

SERVES 4

Beef Choucroute

PREPARATION TIME 25 MINUTES

COOKING TIME 2 HOURS

INGREDIENTS

2 tbsp goose fat or vegetable oil
2 large onions, sliced
2 cloves garlic, finely sliced
2 large carrots, peeled and chopped
200g / 7 oz streaky bacon, diced
3 large floury potatoes, peeled and

cut into chunks
300g / 10 oz / 1 ¼ cups sauerkraut
1 tsp caraway seeds
4 juniper berries, lightly crushed
2 bay leaves
150ml / 5 fl oz / ⅔ cup dry white wine
150ml / 5 fl oz / ⅔ cup chicken stock
2 apples, quartered
2 x sirloin steaks, weighing 225g / 8oz each

- Heat the fat in a large casserole and cook the onions and garlic until golden.
- Add the bacon and cook until the fat starts to render and they begin to crisp.
- Add the potatoes and sauerkraut, stir in the spices, then pour over the wine and stock.
- Cover tightly with a lid and cook gently for 1 hour, stirring occasionally and checking it's not too dry.
- Add the apples and cook for a further 30 minutes.
- Cook the steaks on a griddle for 4 minutes per side, then rest for 5 minutes. Slice thickly and place on top of the choucroute.
- Adjust the seasoning and serve.

255
SERVES 4-6

Beef Carpaccio

PREPARATION TIME 40 MINUTES

INGREDIENTS

250g centre cut beef fillet
Handful rocket (arugula) leaves
Parmesan shavings
1 tbsp capers, drained
Extra virgin olive oil
½ lemon, juiced
Salt and pepper

- Place the fillet in the freezer for 30 minutes to firm it up and make it easier to slice.
- Slice the fillet as thinly as you possibly can with a razor-sharp knife. Place clingfilm over each slice to prevent colouring and use it to stop the slices sticking together. You can keep them this way in the refrigerator until serving.
- 30 minutes before serving remove the beef from the refrigerator and bring up to room temperature.
- Decorate with the rocket, Parmesan and capers and drizzle over the oil and lemon. Season and serve.

Tuna Carpaccio
256

- You can achieve the same effect with fresh tuna steaks for fish lovers.

257
SERVES 4

Stuffed Peppers

PREPARATION TIME 30 MINUTES

COOKING TIME 30 MINUTES

INGREDIENTS

4 ripe red peppers
1 tbsp olive oil
1 onion, peeled and finely chopped
2 cloves garlic, finely chopped
300g / 10 oz / 1 ¼ cups minced beef
1 tbsp rosemary leaves, finely chopped
2 tbsp tomato puree
200g / 7 oz / ¾ cup white rice, cooked
2 tbsp Parmesan, grated

- Cut the tops off the peppers, setting them aside, and hollow out the insides.
- Fry the onion and garlic in the oil until translucent.
- Add the beef and rosemary, turn up the heat and fry briskly, stirring, until the beef is cooked. Season.
- Stir in the tomato puree and a cup of water and leave to simmer until the water is absorbed.
- Stir in the Parmesan and rice and leave to cool a little.
- Preheat the oven to 200°C (180° fan) / 400F / gas 6.
- Fill the peppers with the beef mixture and place in a roasting tin.
- Drizzle with olive oil and bake in the oven for about 30 minutes or until they are soft but retaining their shape.

Stuffed Peppers with Gherkins
258

- Finely chopped gherkins lend a piquancy to the stuffing.

259

SERVES 6

Beef Daube

- Place the meat in a large bowl with the orange zest, bouquet garni. Pepper generously, add a little oil and the red wine. Cover with clingfilm and leave to marinate for 24 hours in the refrigerator.
- The same day, peel the remaining onion, cut in half and push the cloves into it.
- Remove the meat from the marinade, pat dry and add to a casserole in batches to colour on all sides.
- Add the vegetables and cook for 10 minutes until softened then return all the meat to the pan.
- Add the lardons and fry gently, then stir in the tomato puree. Season and cook gently for 10 minutes.
- Add the marinade and its ingredients. Cover and cook over the lowest heat for 3 hours.
- Fish the cloved onion and bouquet garni out of the stew and serve with mashed potato.

Beef Daube with Bulghur Wheat   260

- Serve with bulghur wheat to mop up the juices – lighter than pasta or mash.

PREPARATION TIME 45 MINUTES
+ OVERNIGHT MARINATING

COOKING TIME 3 ½ HOURS

INGREDIENTS

600g / 1 ⅓ lb / 2 ½ cups stewing beef, cubed or 1 large piece if preferred
3 tbsp olive oil
1 orange, grated zest
1 bouquet garni
500ml / 1 pint / 2 cups red wine
2 carrots, peeled and chopped
2 onions, peeled and chopped
3 cloves garlic, peeled and sliced
2 cloves
125g / 4 oz / ½ cup smoked bacon lardons
1 tbsp tomato puree
Salt and pepper

261

SERVES 4

Creole-style Braised Beef Cheeks

- Preheat the oven to 150°C (130° fan) / 300F / gas 2.
- Heat the oil and sear the beef on all sides until golden. Remove with a slotted spoon and set aside.
- Add the onion and peppers and cook until softened, then add the garlic and spices and cook for 2 minutes.
- Add the chillies, stock and tomatoes and bring to a simmer.
- Cover with a lid and cook in the oven for at least 3 hours until the meat is tender stirring occasionally and checking the liquid levels.
- Remove the chillies, adjust the seasoning and serve.

Shin of Beef, Creole Style   262

- If you can't get hold of beef cheeks, chunkily-cut shin of beef will give a similar effect.

PREPARATION TIME 20 MINUTES

COOKING TIME 3 HOURS

INGREDIENTS

1 tbsp vegetable oil
500g / 1 lb / 2 cups beef cheek, cubed
Salt and pepper
1 onion, peeled and chopped
2 green peppers, deseeded and chopped
3 cloves garlic, crushed
2 tbsp curry powder
6 sprigs thyme leaves
1 tsp ground allspice
½ tsp ground cinnamon
2 bay leaves
1-2 Scotch Bonnet chillies
(depending on how hot you want it)
500ml / 1 pint / 2 cups beef stock
1 x 400g can chopped tomatoes

PORK

263 SERVES 6 — Loin of Pork with Apples and Crumble

- Preheat the oven to 200°C (180° fan) / 400F / gas 6.
- Lay the onion slices in a roasting tin and place the pork on top, seasoning and tucking the bay leaves underneath. Drizzle with oil and roast for 1hr 40 minutes.
- Meanwhile, tip the flour into a bowl and rub in the butter using the tips of your fingers until the mixture resembles breadcrumbs. Stir in the hazelnuts and sugar.
- Tip the crumble in an even layer onto a baking sheet and bake until lightly browned – a few minutes.
- Remove the pork from the oven and remove from the tin. Place the tin on the hob and pour in equal quantities wine and water, scraping at the bottom to deglaze. Bubble up and reduce until syrupy.
- Heat the butter in a pan and cook the apple quarters until golden and slightly softened.
- Serve the pork in thick slices with the apple quarters and the crumble sprinkled on top.

PREPARATION TIME 20 MINUTES

COOKING TIME 2 HOURS

INGREDIENTS

1 onion, peeled and thickly sliced
2kg / 4 ½ lb pork loin, boned, derinded and rolled
Olive oil
Bay leaves
1 glass dry white wine

FOR THE CRUMBLE

120g / 4 oz / ½ cup plain (all purpose) flour
100g / 3 ½ oz / ½ cup butter
50g / 1 ¾ oz / ¼ cup crushed hazelnuts (cob nuts)
1 tbsp dark soft brown sugar
4 apples, cored and quartered
2 tbsp butter

Pork Chops & Herbed Potatoes — 264 SERVES 4

PREPARATION TIME 10 MINUTES

COOKING TIME 30 MINUTES

INGREDIENTS

500g / 1 lb / 2 cups salad potatoes, such as Anya or Charlotte
Salt
2 tbsp olive oil
2 sprigs rosemary leaves, chopped
4 pork chops
4 tbsp olive oil
½ lemon, juiced
½ bunch parsley, chopped
1 glass dry white wine, water or chicken stock
½ cucumber, peeled into thin ribbons with a vegetable peeler

- Cook the potatoes in boiling salted water for 20 minutes or until tender.
- Drain thoroughly then set back over the heat to drive off any excess moisture.
- Heat the oil in a large pan. Roughly crush the potatoes with the end of a rolling pin, then tip into the hot oil with the rosemary. Cook until golden and crusty – about 10 minutes.
- Meanwhile heat a frying pan with a little oil. Season the pork chops and cook 2 at a time for 4 minutes per side. Once cooked, squeeze over a little lemon juice and keep warm in a low oven.
- Deglaze the pan with the wine and add in the parsley. Nap over the pork chops and serve with potatoes and cucumber ribbons.

Pork Chops & Sauteed Potatoes — 265 SERVES 4

PREPARATION TIME 15 MINUTES

COOKING TIME 30 MINUTES

INGREDIENTS

500g / 1 lb / 2 cups potatoes, peeled and sliced
2 tbsp goose fat or olive oil
1 clove garlic
Salt and pepper
300g / 10 oz / 1 ¼ cups mushrooms, sliced
½ bunch parsley, chopped
4 pork chops
2 tbsp butter

- Heat the fat in a large frying pan and add the potato slices and garlic. Season and cook over a low heat until golden and crusty.
- Heat the butter in a frying pan and season the pork chops. When foaming add the pork and cook for 4 minutes per side, basting with the butter.
- Set aside to rest.
- Increase the heat under the potato pan and add the mushrooms. Cook until golden and tender then throw in the parsley.
- Serve the pork chops with the potatoes and mushrooms alongside.

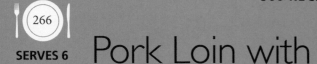

SERVES 6

266

Pork Loin with Caramelised Vegetables

Pork Loin with Pan Juices

267

- Empty the roasting tin, place over a heat and deglaze with cider or white wine.

Roast Pork Loin with Fennel Seeds

268

- Lightly crush 2 tbsp fennel seeds and use to coat the pork before cooking.

Pork Loin with Root Vegetables

269

- Turnips, parsnips and swede would all make good accompaniments roasted around the pork in the same way.

PREPARATION TIME 20 MINUTES

COOKING TIME 1 HOUR 50 MINUTES

....

INGREDIENTS

1 onion, peeled and thickly sliced
2kg / 4 ½ lb pork loin, derinded
2 cloves of garlic, finely chopped
1 tbsp felled seeds, lightly crushed
Salt and pepper
Olive oil
Bay leaves
Rosemary sprigs (leaves plucked)
3 carrots, peeled and chopped into short lengths
2 leeks, chopped into short lengths
8 shallots, whole

- Preheat the oven to 200°C (180° fan) / 400F / gas 6.
- Sprinkle the pork loin with garlic, fennel seeds and plucked rosemary.
- Lay the onion slices in a small roasting tin and place the pork on top, seasoning and tucking the herbs underneath. Tuck the vegetables all around and pour a glass of water into the tin.
- Drizzle with oil and roast for about 1hr 40 minutes.
- Remove the pork from the oven and rest for 10 minutes before carving.
- Increase the oven heat to 220°C (200° fan)/ 450F / gas 7 and brown the vegetables in the tin.
- Squeeze the shallots from their skins. Carve the pork and serve the caramelized vegetables alongside.

270 SERVES 4

Gammon with Pears

- Bring the gammon to room temperature and place in a large pot with the vegetables, peppercorns, bouquet garni and cider. Add enough cold water to cover and bring to a boil.
- Lower the heat to a 'blip' for 30 minutes + 30 minutes per 500g / 1 lb.
- When the ham is cooked, remove from the pan and leave to rest for 10 minutes. Preheat the oven to 200°C (180° fan) / 400F / Gas 7.
- Mix together the oil, honey and mustard. Cover the ham with the mixture and roast in the oven for about 20-30 minutes until golden and caramelised.
- Heat the butter in a pan and when foaming, add the pears cut side down. Caramelise on each side, drizzling over the honey.
- Serve with thick slices of ham.

Gammon with Apples
271

- Substitute apple slices for the pears.

PREPARATION TIME 10 MINUTES

COOKING TIME 2 ½ HOURS

INGREDIENTS

2kg / 4 ½ lb gammon (ham), soaked
to get rid of excess salt
2 carrots, quartered
1 onions, studded with 2 cloves
2 leeks, chopped
10 peppercorns
2 sticks celery, chopped
Bouquet garni
1 L/ 2 ¼ pints / 4 ¼ cups dry cider

4 tbsp honey
4 tbsp grain mustard
2 tbsp olive oil

4 pears, halved and cored
2 tbsp butter
1 tbsp honey

272 SERVES 6

Roast Pork Loin with Confit Onions

- Preheat the oven to 200°C (180° fan) / 400F / gas 6.
- Lay the onion slices in a small roasting tin and place the pork on top, seasoning and tucking the bay leaves underneath. Drizzle with oil and roast for about 1hr 40 minutes.
- Meanwhile melt the butter in a pan and add the onions. Cook very slowly for about 20 minutes until golden.
- Add the sugar, vinegar and a little salt and simmer gently for about 30 minutes until dark and sticky, stirring occasionally.
- Remove the pork from the oven and rest for 10 minutes before carving. Serve with the onion confit.

Roast Pork with Garlic Onion Confit
273

- Add 3-4 whole cloves garlic to the onions for a sweet sticky garlicky flavour.

PREPARATION TIME 20 MINUTES

COOKING TIME 1 HOUR 45 MINUTES

INGREDIENTS

1 onion, peeled and thickly sliced
2kg / 4 ½ lb pork loin, boned, derinded and rolled
Salt and pepper
Olive oil
Bay leaves
1 kg / 2 ¼ lb/ 4 ¼ cups onions, peeled and finely sliced
50g / 1 ¾ oz / ¼ cup butter
100g / 3 ½ oz / ½ cup soft dark brown sugar
3 tbsp red wine vinegar or sherry vinegar
Salt and pepper

274
SERVES 4

Pork Fillet with Summer Vegetables

PREPARATION TIME 10 MINUTES

COOKING TIME 20 MINUTES

INGREDIENTS

1 pork fillet, weighing 750g / 1 ⅓ lb
Salt and pepper
Olive oil
2 tbsp butter
2 handfuls green beans, topped and tailed
1 large handful runner beans, cut into short diamond shapes
2 courgettes (zucchini), cut into matchsticks
½ bunch parsley, finely chopped.

- Preheat the oven to 200°C (180° fan) / 400F / gas 6.
- Place the pork in a roasting tin and season well. Drizzle with oil and roast for 20 minutes until just cooked through.
- Meanwhile heat the butter in a pan and add the vegetables. Pour in a glass of water, cover with a lid and stew gently for 10-15 minutes until all is tender. Season and add the parsley.
- Rest the pork for 5 minutes before carving and serving with the vegetables.

Pork Fillet with Mixed Greens 275

- You can braise hearty winter greens such as kale or cavolo nero in the same way.

276
SERVES 4

Sweet and Sour Pork

PREPARATION TIME 15 MINUTES

COOKING TIME 20 MINUTES

INGREDIENTS

500g / 1 lb pork loin, cubed
1 egg white
2 tsp cornflour
Salt
1 tsp sesame oil
1 tbsp vegetable oil
1 carrot, peeled and cut into matchsticks
1 red pepper, deseeded and finely sliced
50g / 1 ¾ oz / ¼ cup pineapple chunks

FOR THE SAUCE

125ml / 4 fl oz / ½ cup pineapple juice
Splash dry sherry or rice wine
2 tbsp tomato ketchup
2 tbsp soy sauce
2 tbsp Chinese vinegar or red wine vinegar

- Slice the pork into strips. Combine the egg white, cornflour, a pinch of salt and sesame oil in a bowl then thoroughly coat the chicken strips in the mixture.
- Heat the vegetable oil in a wok until smoking, then add the coated pork and stir fry over a high heat until the chicken turns white.
- Remove the pork from the pan and set aside. Discard the oil.
- Heat the oil in the wok again and stir fry the vegetables over a high heat for 4 minutes.
- Mix together the sauce ingredients. Add the pork back to the pan with the sauce, bubble up and serve with white rice.

Sweet Sour Pork Buns 277

- This makes a surprisingly delicious filling for baguette or soft white rolls if you're short of time.

278

SERVES 2

Sausage and Potato Gratin

- Cook the potatoes in boiling salted water until tender. Drain then roughly mash with the butter.
- Heat the oil in a pan and cook the onions until soft and sweet. Add the carrots and cook for a further 10 minutes until soft.
- Add the sausages and cook for another 10 minutes, then pour over the stock and thyme and bubble up.
- Spoon into a gratin dish and season. Top with the roughly mashed potato, then top with smashed potato crisps.
- Grill until golden and bubbling, watching the crisps don't burn.

PREPARATION TIME 15 MINUTES

COOKING TIME 30 MINUTES

INGREDIENTS

2 large floury potatoes, peeled and chopped
2 tbsp butter
2 tbsp vegetable oil
1 onion, thickly sliced
2 carrots, peeled and thickly sliced
4 Cumberland sausages, cut into chunks
200ml / 7 fl oz / ¾ cup chicken stock
1 sprig thyme
Salt and pepper
2 bags crisps (potato chips)

Sausage Celeriac Gratin

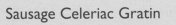 279

- Crushed celeriac can be treated in the same way as the potato.

280

SERVES 4

Sausages with Onion Gravy

- Preheat the oven to 200°C (180° fan) / 400F / gas 6.
- Prick the sausages all over with a fork.
- Drizzle the sausages with oil in a roasting tin and roast for 30 minutes until browned all over, turning occasionally.
- Meanwhile heat the butter in a pan and cook the onions with thyme for 15-20 minutes, until deep gold and sweet.
- Stir in the flour and cook out for 2 minutes, then stir in the wine and stock. Season and simmer for 20 minutes until thickened.
- Stir in the grain mustard, then serve with the cooked sausages and mashed potato.

PREPARATION TIME 10 MINUTES

COOKING TIME 35 MINUTES

INGREDIENTS

8 sausages
Vegetable oil
2 tbsp butter
2 large onions, peeled and thickly sliced
2 sprigs thyme
½ tbsp flour
150ml / 5 fl oz / ⅔ cup Marsala or red wine
400ml / 14 fl oz / 1 ½ cups beef stock
Salt and pepper
1 tbsp grain mustard

TO SERVE
Ultimate mashed potato (see page 82)

Sausages with Sweet Sticky Onion Gravy

 281

- Add 1 tbsp redcurrant jelly or 1 tbsp honey to the onions, but keep the mustard to balance the sweetness.

282

SERVES 4

Pork Chops in Cider

PREPARATION TIME 10 MINUTES

COOKING TIME 30 MINUTES

INGREDIENTS

2 tbsp butter
1 large onion, peeled and thinly sliced
2 apples, peeled, cored and sliced
2 sprigs thyme
1 clove garlic, finely sliced
4 pork chops
Salt and pepper
300ml / 10 fl oz / 1 ¼ cups dry cider
100ml / 3 ½ fl oz / ½ cup double cream (optional)
1 tbsp Dijon mustard

- Heat the butter in a pan and cook the onions and apple with thyme and garlic for 15-20 minutes until all is golden and sweet.
- Remove from the pan with a slotted spoon and increase the heat.
- Sear the pork chops on both sides, seasoning as you go, then lower the heat slightly.
- Return the onions and apples to the pan, pour in the cider, bubble up and cook for 10 minutes.
- Stir in the cream if using and the mustard, adjust the seasoning and serve.

Pork Chops in Beer

283

- A light beer would work the same way as the cider.

284

SERVES 4

Sauteed Pork with Curried Onions

PREPARATION TIME 15 MINUTES

COOKING TIME 30 MINUTES

INGREDIENTS

4 pork escalopes
2 tbsp vegetable oil
2 large onions, peeled and finely sliced
1 red onion, peeled and finely sliced
2 cloves garlic, finely sliced
½ tsp turmeric
1 tsp ground cumin
1 tsp fennel seeds, crushed
1 tsp ground coriander
2 tsp garam masala
200ml / 7 fl oz / ¾ cup chicken stock
Salt and pepper
1 lime, juiced

- Place the pork escalopes between 2 sheets of clingfilm and bat out very thin with a rolling pin. Cut into strips.
- Heat the oil in a pan and cook the onions until deep gold and sweet – about 15-20 minutes.
- Add the garlic and spices and cook for 3 minutes.
- Increase the heat, add the pork strips and sauté until golden.
- Pour in the stock, season and cook until reduced and slightly thickened.
- Serve with the lime squeezed over.

Thai Style Sautéed Pork

285

- Use a red chilli, fish sauce and lime juice in place of the spices to make this a Thai style dish.

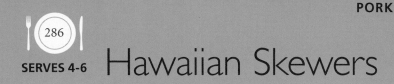

286

SERVES 4-6 # Hawaiian Skewers

**Pork Skewers
with Mango** **287**

- Stoned peeled mango gives a sweet juicy result.

Hawaiian Luxe Skewers **288**

- Alternate the pork cubes and pineapple with chunks of ham, mozzarella and cherry tomatoes for a full-on Hawaiian.

Chicken Kebabs **289**

- Chicken or even rabbit would work well here with the fruit.

PREPARATION TIME 15 MINUTES

COOKING TIME 8-10 MINUTES

INGREDIENTS

800g pork fillet
1 pineapple, skinned and cored, flesh cut into chunks
½ red chilli, deseeded and very finely diced
Salt and pepper
Olive oil
Sweet chilli sauce, to serve

- Cut the pork into bite-size pieces.
- Toss the chunks of pineapple with the chilli.
- Thread the pork and pineapple alternately onto skewers.
- Brush with olive oil and season.
- Heat the barbecue until the coals are glowing and there are no flames.
- Cook the skewers on the grill for about 8 minutes, or until the pork is cooked through.
- Serve alongside sweet chilli sauce.

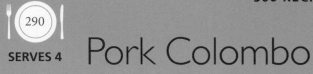

290 SERVES 4

Pork Colombo

Rabbit Colombo
291
- Rabbit or chicken for the faint hearted would suit this quick stew.

Mild Pork Colombo
292
- If scotch bonnet chillies are too hot, try a softer fruitier type such as jalapeno.

Pork Colombo with Spinach
293
- Try stirring baby spinach leaves through the stew just before serving.

PREPARATION TIME 20 MINUTES

COOKING TIME 45 MINUTES

INGREDIENTS

1 tbsp vegetable oil
500g / 1 lb / 2 cups pork loin, cubed
Salt and pepper
1 onion, peeled and chopped
2 green peppers, deseeded and chopped
3 cloves garlic, crushed
2 tbsp curry powder
6 sprigs thyme leaves
1 tsp ground allspice
½ tsp ground cinnamon
2 bay leaves
1-2 Scotch Bonnet chillies
(depending on how hot you want it)
750g / 1 ⅓ lb sweet potatoes, peeled and cubed
500ml / 1 pint / 2 cups chicken stock
1 x 400g can chopped tomatoes

- Heat the oil and sear the pork on all sides until golden. Remove with a slotted spoon and set aside.
- Add the onion and peppers and cook until softened, then add the garlic and spices and cook for 2 minutes.
- Add the chillies, sweet potatoes, stock and tomatoes and bring to a simmer.
- Reduce the heat, cover with a lid and cook for 20 minutes until the potatoes are tender.
- Add the pork back to the pan and simmer for 10 minutes until cooked.
- Remove the chillies, adjust the seasoning and serve.

294

SERVES 4

Breaded Pork Chops

- Trim the thick white fat from around the pork chops. Place between 2 pieces of clingfilm and bat out with a rolling pin until about half as thick.
- Lay the flour, egg, breadcrumbs with oregano and mustard powder and seasoning in separate bowls.
- Dip the pork chops into each bowl in turn, thoroughly coating each time.
- Heat a thin layer of oil in a pan and cook the chops 2 at a time for 5 minutes per side until golden. Keep warm in a low oven while you cook the remaining chops.
- Serve with lemon wedges.

PREPARATION TIME 15 MINUTES

COOKING TIME 20 MINUTES

....

INGREDIENTS

4 pork chops
1 egg, beaten
4 tbsp flour
100g / 3 ½ oz / ½ cup fine breadcrumbs
1 tsp dried oregano
1 tsp mustard powder
Salt and pepper
Vegetable oil
Lemon wedges

Herby Pork Chops

 295

- Finely chop rosemary, parsley and thyme with the breadcrumbs.

296

SERVES 4

Pork Fillet with Creamy Munster Sauce

- Preheat the oven to 200°C (180° fan) / 400F / gas 6.
- Place the pork in a roasting tin, season, drizzle with oil and roast for 18 minutes, until just pink in the centre.
- Meanwhile heat the butter in a pan and sweat the shallots until translucent.
- Add the garlic and thyme and cook for 3 minutes.
- Add the wine, bubble up and reduce until about 1 tbsp is left in the bottom, then add the cream.
- Bubble up, then stir in the cheese until melted. Adjust the seasoning.
- Rest the pork for 5 minutes before slicing and serving with the creamy sauce.

PREPARATION TIME 10 MINUTES

COOKING TIME 20 MINUTES

....

INGREDIENTS

1 pork tenderloin, weighing 750g / 1 ⅓ lb
30g / 1 oz butter
1 tbsp oil
2 shallots, finely chopped
1 clove garlic, finely sliced
2 sprigs thyme
150ml / 5 fl oz / ⅔ cup dry white wine
300ml / 10 fl oz / 1 ¼ cup double cream
80g / 2 ½ oz / ⅓ cup Munster cheese, cubed
Salt and pepper

Pork Fillet with Creamy Blue Sauce

 297

- If Munster is too strong, try a melting gorgonzola dolce.

LAMB

298
SERVES 4
Lamb in Milk Sauce

- Preheat the oven to 180°C (160° fan) / 350F / gas 5.
- Place the lamb in a casserole and make small deep cuts all over.
- Mix the butter with the herbs, garlic and a pinch of salt and push into the cuts on the lamb.
- Cover with a lid and bake in the oven for about 30 minutes.
- Remove the lid and cook for a further 20 minutes, then pour over the milk and cook for 30 minutes. The milk will set into 'curds' and form a sauce.
- Leave to rest for 10 minutes before serving with steamed potatoes.

PREPARATION TIME 15 MINUTES

COOKING TIME 1 HOUR 20 MINUTES

INGREDIENTS

1 leg of lamb, weighing about 1.5 kg / 3 lb
50g / 1 ¾ oz / ¼ cup butter
½ bunch sage leaves, chopped
1 tbsp thyme leaves
3 cloves garlic, crushed
300ml / 10 fl. oz / 1 ¼ cups milk
Extra virgin olive oil

299
SERVES 4
Irish Stew

PREPARATION TIME 15 MINUTES

COOKING TIME 6 HOURS

INGREDIENTS

55 ml / 2 fl. oz / 1/4 cup sunflower oil
450 g / 1 lb / 3 cups lamb shoulder, diced
300 g / 10 ½ oz / 2 cups new potatoes, peeled and sliced
2 carrots, peeled and sliced
2 onions, chopped
1 tbsp juniper berries, lightly crushed
2-3 bay leaves

500 ml / 18 fl. oz / 2 cups lamb stock
salt and pepper

TO GARNISH
1 tbsp curly leaf parsley leaves, finely chopped

- Heat half of the oil in a large casserole dish set over a moderate heat until hot.
- Season the lamb generously and seal in batches until golden brown in colour all over.
- Transfer the sealed lamb to a slow cooker and reduce the heat under the casserole dish a little.
- Add the remaining oil and saute the onions and carrots for 4-5 minutes, stirring occasionally.
- Add the bay leaves, potatoes, juniper berries, stock and a little seasoning and stir well.
- Pour on top of the lamb in the slow cooker and stir thoroughly.
- Cover and cook on a medium setting for 6 hours.
- Adjust the seasoning to taste after 6 hours and ladle the stew into serving dishes.
- Garnish with the chopped parsley before serving.

300
SERVES 4
Lamb stuffed with Pancetta

PREPARATION TIME 20 MINUTES

COOKING TIME 2 HOURS

INGREDIENTS

1 leg of lamb, tunnel boned (ask your butcher)
120ml / 4 fl. oz / ½ cup white wine
2 bay leaves
2 cloves garlic, whole

FOR THE STUFFING
2 tbsp olive oil
4 slices pancetta, diced
1 onion, peeled and finely chopped
1 cloves garlic, finely chopped
1 sprig rosemary, finely chopped
2 tbsp black olives, chopped
5 sage leaves, finely chopped

- Preheat the oven to 200°C (180° fan) / 400F / gas 6.
- Make the stuffing: heat the oil in a pan and cook the pancetta till the fat runs and it starts to turn crisp.
- Add the onion, garlic and rosemary and cook until soft and golden. Add the olives, sage and season carefully.
- Lay the lamb in a roasting tin and stuff the tunnelled-out section with the stuffing using a teaspoon. Seal the ends with toothpicks or skewers.
- Pour equal amounts wine and water into the roasting tin with the bay leaves and garlic. Season the lamb, tent with foil and cook for about 1 ½ - 2 hours until meltingly tender.
- Leave for 15 minutes before carving.

Redcurrant-Glazed Lamb Cutlets

Mixed Currant Glazed Cutlets 302

- Use the same quantity of mixed red, white and blackcurrants, whizzed in a blender for the marinade along with the port.

Lamb Cutlets with Mustard Redcurrant Glaze 303

- Adding a tbsp wholegrain mustard adds heat without fire.

Lamb Cutlets with Flageolet Beans 304

- Instead of the usual potatoes, try serving with warm flageolet beans as a classic accompaniment.

PREPARATION TIME 10 MINUTES

COOKING TIME 12 MINUTES

INGREDIENTS

2 racks of lamb, trimmed

FOR THE GLAZE
230g / 8 oz / 1 cup redcurrant jelly
1 sprig thyme
100ml / 3 ½ fl. oz / ½ cup port or cassis
1 sprig rosemary

- Preheat the oven to 180°C / 350F / gas 5.
- Warm the jelly, port and thyme in a small pan and reduce until thickened and syrupy.
- Using the rosemary, brush the glaze onto the lamb racks in a roasting tin and season.
- Cook for about 12 minutes, glazing once again half way through, then remove from the oven and rest for 5 minutes before carving.
- Serve with the remaining sauce.

305

SERVES 4

Marinated Lamb Kebabs

- Toss the cubed lamb with the garlic, balsamic, rosemary, a little oil and salt and pepper and leave to marinate for up to 30 minutes.
- Thread the lamb onto skewers, alternating with the tomatoes, peppers and onion. Sprinkle a little seasoning over.
- Cook over hot embers for 8-10 minutes until the lamb is rose pink inside and charred outside

PREPARATION TIME 35 MINUTES

COOKING TIME 10 MINUTES

INGREDIENTS

500g lamb fillet or leg steak, cut into 2cm cubes
2 cloves garlic, crushed
2 tbsp balsamic vinegar
1 tbsp rosemary leaves, chopped
Olive oil
Salt and pepper
16 cherry tomatoes
8 mild red chilli peppers, whole
1 onion, cut into chunks

Spanish Style Kebabs

306

- Whizz together 1 tbsp smoked paprika, a handful bottled roasted peppers, 2 cloves garlic and a splash of dry sherry in a food blender until smooth for an alternative.

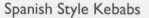

307

SERVES 4

Roast Shoulder of Lamb with Thyme

- Preheat the oven to 180°C / 350F / gas 5.
- Place the shoulder in a tin and rub in the herbs, oil, honey and seasoning, massaging them into the meat.
- Pour a glass of water or wine into the bottom of the tin, cover tightly with foil and bake for about 2-3 hours until the lamb is meltingly tender and falls from the bone.
- Allow to rest for a few minutes before 'carving.'

PREPARATION TIME 10 MINUTES

COOKING TIME 2-3 HOURS

INGREDIENTS

1 lamb shoulder weighing 1.5kg / 3 lb
1 bunch thyme leaves
1 tbsp oregano
4 tbsp olive oil
2 tbsp runny honey
Salt and pepper
Water or red wine

Shoulder of Lamb with Lavender

308

- In the summer use dried lavender heads in place of the thyme.

309
SERVES 4

Griddled Lamb with Feta Salad

PREPARATION TIME 15 MINUTES

COOKING TIME 5-10 MINUTES

....

INGREDIENTS

4 lamb leg steaks
2 tbsp Balsamic vinegar
1 tbsp marjoram leaves
Salt and pepper
Olive oil
150g / 5 oz / ⅔ cup feta, crumbled
4 ripe tomatoes, chopped
½ cucumber, diced
2 handfuls black olives
Salad leaves
Extra virgin olive oil
½ lemon, juiced

- Marinade the lamb in the balsamic, herbs, oil and a little seasoning.
- Heat a griddle until nearly smoking and cook 3 minutes per side for pink lamb.
- Place on foil and wrap up; leave to rest for 5 minutes.
- Meanwhile assemble the salad on a large platter, scattering the ingredients on.
- Toss with oil, lemon juice and a little seasoning and mix with your hands.
- Lay the lamb and its resting juices on the salad and serve.

Lamb with Middle Eastern Salad   310

- Mix a can of drained chickpeas with the salad ingredients and add thyme leaves and a little dried chilli.

311
SERVES 4

Moroccan Lamb Meatballs

PREPARATION TIME 50 MINUTES

COOKING TIME 15 MINUTES

....

INGREDIENTS

500g / 1 lb / 2 cups minced lamb
1 onion, very finely chopped
2 cloves garlic, finely chopped
6 tbsp breadcrumbs
1 tbsp tomato puree
1 tsp ground cinnamon
1 tsp ground cumin
½ lemon, juiced
Salt and pepper
2 tbsp olive oil

- Place the minced lamb in a large bowl and bring to room temperature.
- Add the rest of the ingredients and mix well with your hands to ensure even distribution.
- Roll the mixture into small walnut-sized balls with your hands and place on a baking sheet. Cover with clingfilm and refrigerate for 30 minutes.
- Heat the olive oil in a large pan.
- Add the meatballs in batches, cooking on all sides until golden and just cooked through – about 6-8 minutes.

Meatballs in Broth   312

- Serve in hot strong chicken stock with rice alongside for a filling supper.

313

SERVES 4

Spicy Lamb Kebabs

- Pat the cubes of lamb dry with kitchen paper.
- Whiz the ingredients for the marinade in a food processor until smooth.
- Toss the lamb in the paste and leave to marinate in the refrigerator for at least 1 hour or overnight.
- Thread the lamb onto skewers and cook either on a barbecue or very hot griddle pan until charred on the outside and pink in the centre – about 5-6 minutes.

PREPARATION TIME 10 MINUTES
+ MARINADING TIME

COOKING TIME 5-6 MINUTES

....

INGREDIENTS

500g / 1 lb / 2 cups lamb, cut into cubes

FOR THE MARINADE
½ onion, peeled and chopped
2-3 green chillies, deseeded if preferred and chopped
3 cloves garlic, peeled
2 tsp fresh ginger, chopped
1 tsp ground cumin
1 tsp ground coriander
1 tbsp dried mint
4 tbsp plain yoghurt
Salt

Tikka Style Kebabs   314

- Add 1 tbsp tomato puree to the marinade.

315

SERVES 4

Lamb Cassoulet

- Rinse the beans and place in a pan covered with cold water. Bring to a simmer and cook for 2 hours or until soft.
- Preheat the oven to 160°C (140° fan) / 325F / gas 4.
- Add the oil to a casserole and render the fat from the bacon. Add the onions and garlic and cook until browned.
- Add the lamb and cook on all sides, then add the tomatoes and stock and herbs. Add the drained beans, cover with a lid and cook in the oven for 2 ½ hours, stirring the beans to disturb the crust every 30 minutes.
- Remove the lid for the last 30 minutes of cooking and scatter with the breadcrumbs to create a crust.
- Serve hot with a crisp salad.

PREPARATION TIME 30 MINUTES

COOKING TIME 2 HOURS 30 MINUTES

....

INGREDIENTS

350g / 12 oz / 1 ½ cups dried cannellini beans (or traditional Tarbais beans), soaked overnight
750g / 1 ⅓ lb / 3 cups boneless stewing lamb, cubed
2 rashers smoked streaky bacon, diced
1 tbsp oil
2 onions, peeled and chopped
3 cloves garlic, chopped
1 x 400g can chopped tomatoes
500ml / 1 pint / 2 cups chicken stock
Bouquet garni
Salt and pepper
3 handfuls breadcrumbs

Toulouse-Style Cassoulet   316

- Some good quality lamb and mint sausages make an excellent addition if you can find them.

POULTRY

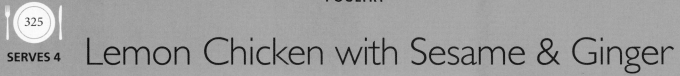

Lemon Chicken with Sesame & Ginger

325

SERVES 4

- Slice the chicken into strips.
- Combine the egg white, cornflour, a pinch of salt and sesame oil in a bowl then thoroughly coat the chicken strips in the mixture.
- Heat the vegetable oil in a wok until smoking, then add the coated chicken and stir fry over a high heat until the chicken turns white.
- Remove the chicken from the pan and set aside. Discard the oil.
- Add the ginger, lemon juice and zest, stock, sugar and soy and sherry/wine and bring to a rapid boil.
- Whisk in the cornflour until thickened then return the chicken to the pan for a few minutes to cook through. Scatter over the sesame seeds
- Taste the sauce – you may want more lemon, sugar or salt. Serve alongside long grain rice.

PREPARATION TIME 10 MINUTES

COOKING TIME 15 MINUTES

INGREDIENTS

2 tbsp vegetable oil
1 tbsp fresh ginger, grated
3-4 lemons, grated zest and juice
100ml chicken stock
1-2 tsp sugar
Splash soy sauce
Splash dry sherry
1 tsp cornflour
1 tbsp sesame seeds

FOR THE LEMON CHICKEN
4 chicken breasts, skinned
1 egg white
2 tsp cornflour
1 tsp sesame oil

Roast Chicken with Sage Butter

326

SERVES 4-6

PREPARATION TIME 15 MINUTES

COOKING TIME 1 HOUR 30 MINUTES

INGREDIENTS

1 chicken
Olive oil

FOR THE BUTTER
6 sage leaves, finely chopped
150g / 5 oz / ⅔ cup butter, softened
Salt and pepper
½ lemon, grated zest

- Preheat the oven to 200°C (180° fan) / 400F / gas 6.
- Place the chicken in a roasting tin. Using the handle of a teaspoon, gently loosen the skin from the meat, using the spoon to create pockets.
- Mix the butter with the sage, seasoning and lemon zest.
- Push the butter into the pockets under the skin, using your fingers to massage it out and cover the breast.
- Drizzle the skin with oil and season, then roast in the oven for 20 minutes + 20 minutes per 500g/1 lb. The chicken is cooked when the juices run clear at the thickest part.
- Leave to rest for 10 minutes before carving.

Stuffed Roast Pheasant

327

SERVES 2-4

PREPARATION TIME 15 MINUTES

COOKING TIME 30-40 MINUTES

INGREDIENTS

1 pheasant, cleaned and boned out (ask your butcher)

FOR THE STUFFING
250g / 9 oz / 1 cup mild goats' cheese
2 tbsp parsley, finely chopped
1 tbsp thyme leaves
1 clove garlic, crushed
Salt and pepper

- Preheat oven to 200°C (180° fan) / 400F / gas 6.
- Lay the pheasant out on a surface and open it out.
- Mix together the stuffing ingredients, then spread the stuffing out into the cavity of the bird.
- Season, then roll the bird up into a rough sausage shape and secure with string.
- Place in a roasting tin and season, drizzle with oil and roast for 30-40 minutes until cooked through and the juices run clear.
- Leave to rest for 10 minutes before carving.

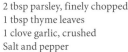

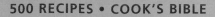

328

SERVES 4

Chicken Fajitas

PREPARATION TIME 35 MINUTES

COOKING TIME 10-15 MINUTES

INGREDIENTS

2 chicken breasts, skinned and thinly sliced
2 tsp paprika
2 tsp ground cumin
2 tsp ground coriander
Pinch dried chilli flakes
Salt and pepper
4 tbsp olive oil
1 onion, peeled and finely sliced
1 red pepper, deseeded and finely sliced
1 green pepper, deseeded and finely sliced
4 tbsp canned sweetcorn
1 lime, juiced
8 tortilla wraps
Sour cream
Tomato salsa
Guacamole

- Coat the chicken in half the spices and leave to marinate for 30 minutes.
- Heat half the oil in a pan until nearly smoking, then cook the onion and peppers until golden and tender. Remove from the pan, keep warm and set aside.
- Add the remaining oil and reheat, then add the meat and sprinkle over the remaining spices.
- Stir briskly for 2-3 minutes until either the chicken is cooked through. Mix in the sweetcorn and squeeze over the lime juice. Remove and keep warm.
- Wipe out the pan and use to warm the tortillas through.
- Serve the vegetables with the meat, tortilla wraps and sauces.

Steak Fajitas

329

- Thinly sliced rump steak makes a luxury substitute.

330

SERVES 4

Chicken with Herbs and Lemon

PREPARATION TIME 5 MINUTES

COOKING TIME 25-30 MINUTES

INGREDIENTS

4 chicken breasts
Handful mixed thyme, rosemary, parsley
Salt and pepper
4 tbsp olive oil
2 preserved lemons
200ml / 7 fl. oz / ¾ cup water, white wine or chicken stock

- Preheat the oven to 200°C (180° fan) / 400F / gas 6.
- Place the chicken snugly in a roasting tin and tuck the herbs in and around the meat.
- Season and drizzle over the oil, then slice the lemons and tuck around the meat.
- Pour over the stock and bake for 25 – 30 minutes or until the chicken is cooked through and the juices run clear.
- Remove the chicken to a warm place to rest. Squish the lemons against the side of the tin and stir into the cooking juices.
- Serve the chicken with the cooking juices poured over.

Citrus Chicken

331

- If you can't get hold of preserved lemons, simply use 1 quartered lemon and ½ orange if desired

332
SERVES 4-6
Chicken Liver and Port Paté

- Heat a tbsp of butter in a frying pan and cook the chicken livers over a medium heat for 5 minutes, turning them frequently, until golden brown without and just pink within.
- Transfer with a slotted spoon to a food processor, reserving the frying pan and juices.
- Pour the port into the pan, scraping with a wooden spoon and add to the processor.
- Melt 150g butter and pour into the processor. Add the mace, thyme, garlic and salt and pepper. Blend to a smooth puree.
- Spoon into a pot or individual ramekins. Melt the remaining butter and pour over, leave to cool then chill for 24 hours before serving with hot toast.

PREPARATION TIME 20 MINUTES

COOKING TIME 5 MINUTES

INGREDIENTS

225g / 8 oz / 1 cup chicken livers, trimmed
225g / 8 oz / 1 cup butter, softened
2 tbsp port
¼ tsp ground mace
1 tsp thyme leaves
1 clove garlic, crushed
Salt and pepper

Chicken Liver Cognac Pate
333
- The same quantity of cognac gives a less sweet taste.

334
SERVES 4
Chicken Kiev

- Using a sharp knife, cut a pocket in the side of each chicken breast.
- Mix together the stuffing ingredients until well combined.
- Use a teaspoon to stuff the pocket with the herb butter, then press the edges firmly together.
- Place the flour, eggs and breadcrumbs on separate plates. Season the flour.
- Dip each chicken breast into the flour, eggs then polenta, coating thoroughly each time.
- Heat the oil then add the chicken breasts and cook, turning regularly for about 20 minutes until cooked through.

PREPARATION TIME 10 MINUTES

COOKING TIME 20 MINUTES

INGREDIENTS

4 chicken breasts, skinned
75g / 2 ¾ oz / ⅓ cup plain
(all purpose) flour
3 eggs, beaten
250g / 9 oz / 1 cup breadcrumbs
4 tbsp vegetable oil
Salt and pepper

FOR THE STUFFING
225g / 8 oz / 1 cup butter, softened
2-3 cloves garlic, crushed
½ bunch parsley, finely chopped
½ bunch tarragon, finely chopped
Squeeze of lemon juice

Pork Fillet Kiev
335
- Batted out pork fillets will give a similar result.

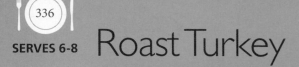

336

SERVES 6-8 # Roast Turkey

Herb Butter-Basted Turkey

337

- Use a teaspoon handle to separate the skin from the flesh and stuff the pockets with softened butter mixed with finely chopped parsley.

Citrus Turkey

338

- Season the butter with lemon zest and plenty of black pepper before rubbing on the bird.

Paprika Turkey

339

- Sprinkle smoked paprika over the turkey for a fuller flavour and a really golden colour.

PREPARATION TIME 10 MINUTES

COOKING TIME 2-3 HOURS

INGREDIENTS

1 turkey, weighing 5.4-6.3kg / 12-14 lb at room temperature
200g / 7 oz / ¾ cup butter, softened or goose fat
Salt and pepper
8-10 rashers smoked streaky bacon

- Preheat the oven to 200°C (180° fan) / 400F / gas 6.
- Rub the turkey all over with the butter or goose fat, season and cover with the smoked bacon.
- Place in the oven and roast for 30 minutes, then reduce the heat to 180°C (160° fan) / 350F / gas 4 and cook for a further 2 hours or so, until the juices run clear at the thickest part.
- Leave to rest for 30 minutes before carving.

340

SERVES 4

Tandoori Chicken

- Prepare the tandoori marinade by mixing together all the ingredients for the marinade in a mixing bowl. Add the chicken, mix well, then cover and chill for at least 1 hour.
- Bring the water to the boil in a large saucepan and add the rice. Bring back to the boil, then cover and simmer for 10-12 minutes.
- Remove from the heat and keep the lid in place and set to one side.
- Pre-heat the grill to hot. Remove the chicken from the marinade, shaking off any excess, and thread onto the wooden skewers.
- Grill for 8-10 minutes, turning occasionally until lightly charred and cooked through.
- Place the tandoori chicken skewers on top and garnish with the finely diced tomato, sprigs of coriander and a sprinkle of ground cinnamon before serving.

Tandoori Chicken in Pitta Breads   341

- Heat and split pitta breads and fill with the tandoori chicken.

PREPARATION TIME 90 MINUTES

COOKING TIME 30 MINUTES

INGREDIENTS

4 skinless chicken breasts, diced
200ml / 7 fl. oz / ¾ cup basmati rice (use a measuring jug), rinsed
400ml / 14 fl. oz / 1 ½ cups boiling water
½ salad tomato, finely diced
Salt and pepper
Pinch of ground cinnamon
Sprigs of coriander (cilantro)
Wooden skewers, soaked in water

FOR THE MARINADE

300ml/10 fl. oz/1 ¼ cups natural yoghurt
1 tsp ground cumin
1 tsp ground coriander
1 tsp garam masala
1 tsp ground cinnamon
1 ½ tsp tandoori chilli powder
1 tsp caster (superfine) sugar
1 clove garlic, minced

342

SERVES 2

Pheasant with Pears and Sage Butter

- Place the pheasant in a roasting tin. Using the handle of a teaspoon, gently loosen the skin from the meat, using the spoon to create pockets.
- Mix the butter with the sage, seasoning and lemon zest.
- Push the butter into the pockets under the skin, using your fingers to massage it out and cover the breast.
- Place in the oven and roast for 20 minutes, then reduce the heat to 180°C / 350F and cook for another 20-25 minutes, until the juices run clear. Cover with foil if it looks like it might burn.
- 15 minutes before the end of cooking, add the pears to the tin, drizzle with honey, then return to the oven to finish cooking.
- Leave to rest, breast-side down for 10 minutes before serving.

Pheasant with Smoky Bacon Lardons   343

- Scatter smokey bacon lardons over the pears before returning to the oven.

PREPARATION TIME 15 MINUTES

COOKING TIME 40 MINUTES

INGREDIENTS

1 pheasant, cleaned
Olive oil
2 pears, halved and cored
1 tbsp honey

FOR THE BUTTER

6 sage leaves, finely chopped
150g / 5 oz / ⅔ cup butter, softened
Salt and pepper
½ lemon, grated zest

344

SERVES 4

Breaded Chicken Escalopes

PREPARATION TIME 20 MINUTES

COOKING TIME 8-10 MINUTES

....

INGREDIENTS

4 chicken breasts, skinned
1 ball mozzarella, sliced
Salt and pepper
3 tbsp flour
2 eggs, beaten
200g / 6 ½ oz / ¾ cup breadcrumbs
Olive oil
Cherry tomatoes, halved

- Place the chicken between 2 pieces of clingfilm and bat out until a bit thinner with a rolling pin.
- Using a sharp knife, cut a pocket into the side of each chicken.
- Stuff the pocket with mozzarella and close the edges of the chicken back over to enclose the cheese.
- Season, then dunk each pieces into flour, then egg then the breadcrumbs.
- Heat the oil in a large pan and fry until golden and crisp and the chicken cooked through – 8-10 minutes.
- Add the halved tomatoes to the pan and cook until just collapsing. Serve with the chicken.

Breaded Chicken with Taleggio Cheese

345

- Taleggio used in place of the mozzarella will give a stronger flavour.

346

SERVES 4

Coq au Vin

PREPARATION TIME 20 MINUTES

COOKING TIME 1 HOUR

....

INGREDIENTS

50g / 1 ¾ oz / ¼ cup butter
6 rashers smoked streaky bacon or pancetta, diced
2 onions, peeled and finely sliced
3 cloves garlic, finely sliced
2 sprigs thyme
1 chicken, jointed
2 tbsp seasoned flour
300g / 10 oz / 1 ¼ cups chestnut mushrooms, quartered
600ml / 1 pint / 2 cups medium white wine, such as Riesling
300ml / 10 fl. oz / 1 ½ cups double cream
Salt and pepper
2 tbsp parsley, chopped
Squeeze of lemon juice

- Heat the butter in a casserole and fry the bacon until starting to colour.
- Add the onion and garlic and cook until lightly gold. Add the thyme.
- Using a slotted spoon, remove the bacon and onions from the pan to a bowl.
- Add a little oil. Lightly dust the chicken joints with flour, shake off any excess and brown on all sides in the pan.
- Add the mushrooms and cook until golden, then return the bacon and onions to the pan.
- Pour over the wine, bubble up and cook gently for about 30 minutes until the chicken is cooked through.
- Pour in the cream and parsley, season and add a little lemon juice. Heat until the cream starts to thicken, then serve.

Coq Au Vin Rouge

347

- Use red wine in place of the white wine and omit the cream for a punchier dish.

348
SERVES 8
Foie Gras Terrine

- Rinse the foie gras and pat dry. Open the lobes up gently with your fingers and find the large vein that splits up and reaches like tributaries into the lobe.
- Carefully pull out all these veins, using a small sharp knife if necessary and trying to keep the lobes as intact as possible.
- Push the two lobes back together then place in a bowl with the wine, sugar and salt. Leave for 3 hours.
- Line a terrine mould with cling film, then push the marinated foie gras into the mould and place weights on top.
- Press overnight in the refrigerator.
- The next day unmould and slice and serve with brioche and chutney.
- If desired you could very briefly, over a very high heat, flash fry it on each side to heat through.

PREPARATION TIME 3 ½ HOURS + PRESSING TIME

INGREDIENTS

1 lobe of foie gras at room temperature
400ml / 14 fl. oz / 1 ½ cups dessert wine such as Sauternes
60g / 2 oz / ¼ cup salt
30g / 1 oz sugar

TO SERVE
Toasted brioche
Fruit chutney

Foie Gras Terrine with Steak
349

- Serve a very fine slice to melt on top of ribeye steak.

350
SERVES 4
Peking Duck

- Place the duck on a wire rack skin side up and dry thoroughly with kitchen paper. Score the skins with a sharp knife.
- Mix together the ingredients and brush the skin and leave to marinate for about 30 minutes.
- Preheat the oven to 190°C (170° fan) / 375F / gas 5.
- Brush the duck all over with the sauce and transfer the wire rack to a roasting tin. Pour a cup of water into the bottom of the tin and roast/steam for 30 minutes until the duck is cooked through and the skin is crisp.
- You can quickly grill the skin if it hasn't crisped up.
- Serve with rice or pancakes.

PREPARATION TIME 35 MINUTES

COOKING TIME 30 MINUTES

INGREDIENTS

4 duck breasts
2 tbsp runny honey
2 tbsp rice vinegar
1 ½ tbsp soy sauce
1 tbsp Chinese 5 spice
1 tbsp soft dark brown sugar

Chilli Peking Duck
351

- Crushed Szechuan peppercorns will add their distinctive lip-numbing tingling heat to the marinade.

FISH AND SHELLFISH

Littleneck Clams with Garlic & Parsley

352

SERVES 2

- Place the clams in a large bowl of cold water to get rid of any sand.
- Heat the oil and sweat the shallot and garlic until translucent.
- Add the chilli and cook for 1 minute, then toss in the clams, discarding any that remain open when tapped.
- Pour over the white wine, stir in the parsley and cover with a lid and steam for 5-8 minutes until all have opened.
- Discard any that remain closed, season and ladle into bowls, leaving the very bottom of the cooking liquor which will be sandy.

PREPARATION TIME 5 MINUTES

COOKING TIME 10 MINUTES

INGREDIENTS

500g/ 1 lb / 2 cups littleneck clams
2 tbsp olive oil
1 shallot, finely chopped
2 cloves garlic, finely chopped
1 red chilli, deseeded and finely chopped (optional)
200ml / 7 fl. oz / ¾ cup dry white wine
Salt and pepper
½ lemon, juiced
1 bunch flat leaf parsley, finely chopped

Pan-fried Scallops with Leeks

353

SERVES 4

PREPARATION TIME 10 MINUTES

COOKING TIME 10-15 MINUTES

INGREDIENTS

50g / 1 ¾ oz / ¼ cup butter
2 leeks, white part only, finely sliced
30g / 1 oz butter
12 scallops, cleaned and trimmed

Salt and pepper
½ lemon, juiced

- Heat the butter in a pan and when foaming add the leeks. Cook very gently for at least 10 minutes until soft and sweet.
- Heat the 30g butter in another pan and when foaming add the scallops. Cook for 90 seconds on one side and when golden, turn over and cook the other side. Remove from the heat and rest briefly.
- Season the leeks and spoon onto plates. Top with the scallops, squeeze over a little lemon juice and seasoning and serve.

Oysters with Herb Sauce

354

SERVES 4

PREPARATION TIME 5 MINUTES

INGREDIENTS

16 oysters, opened
1 bunch parsley, chopped
1 clove garlic, chopped
75ml / 2 ½ fl. oz / ⅓ cup olive oil
1 lemon, grated zest
Salt and pepper

- Place the opened oysters on a platter of crushed ice.
- Whiz the parsley, garlic, oil and zest in a food processor until the consistency of pesto. Loosen with more oil if necessary.
- Taste – it may need lemon juice as well as seasoning.
- Spoon a little of the sauce on top of each oyster.

355

SERVES 2

Mussels Marinière

PREPARATION TIME 10 MINUTES

COOKING TIME 10 MINUTES

INGREDIENTS

1kg / 2 lb / 4 ¼ cups mussels, scrubbed and de-bearded
1 tbsp olive oil
1 onion, peeled and very finely chopped
4 cloves garlic, finely chopped
1 stick celery, finely chopped
300ml / 10 fl. oz / 1 ½ cups dry white wine
Salt and pepper

- Wash the mussels in a bowl of deep cold water. Discard any that remain open when tapped.
- Heat the oil in a large pot and gently fry the onion, garlic and celery until softened.
- Drain the shellfish and add to the pot then toss in the white wine and bubble up.
- Cover with a lid, shake the pot a little and leave the shellfish to open – about 8-10 minutes.
- When they are all just open, taste the sauce and adjust the seasoning if necessary.
- Serve in deep bowls.

Mussels with Cider   356

- Use cider in place of the wine.

357

SERVES 4

Red Snapper with Deep Fried Leeks

PREPARATION TIME 10 MINUTES

COOKING TIME 10 MINUTES

INGREDIENTS

2 tbsp olive oil
4 red snapper fillets, boned
Salt and pepper
½ lemon, juiced
2 leeks, white part only, very finely sliced lengthways
Vegetable oil for deep frying
Rocket (arugula) to serve

- Heat the oil in a pan and when very hot add the fish fillets skin side down.
- Cook for 2-3 minutes, depending on thickness, then carefully turn over and cook the other side for about 1 minute. Remove from the pan and keep warm.
- Heat the vegetable oil to 180°C / 350F then drop in the leeks a handful at a time until they turn golden and crisp. Remove to drain on kitchen paper.
- Lay the snapper fillets on a thin bed of rocket and squeeze over some lemon juice and a little salt. Top with the deep fried leeks and serve.

Monkfish Tail with Leeks   358

- Monkfish tails are meaty and sweet and would go well with the leeks.

359

SERVES 4

Steamed Halibut with Onions Two Ways

- Heat the butter in a pan and cook the onions over a very low heat for at least 20 minutes until golden and very sweet.
- Place the halibut on a plate in a steamer, season and cook for about 10 minutes or until the fish is just cooked through and a flake comes away easily.
- Serve the halibut on top of the golden onions, topped with spring onions.

PREPARATION TIME 10 MINUTES

COOKING TIME 30 MINUTES

INGREDIENTS

40g / 1 ½ oz butter
1 onion, peeled and finely sliced
4 thick slices halibut
Salt and pepper
½ bunch spring onions (scallions) finely sliced

Halibut with Red and White Onions

360

- Use 1 red onion as well as the white onion to add to the colour.

361

MAKES 20-24

Caribbean Haddock Fritters

- Add the yeast to the water with the sugar, stir well and set aside for 10 minutes until it starts to foam.
- Whisk the flour, baking powder, pepper and allspice together, then stir in the yeast mixture and milk and make a smooth batter.
- Flake in the haddock and stir to coat, then stir in the remaining flavourings. Leave to rest for 2 hours.
- Heat the oil to 180°C / 350F and drop in the batter using a tablespoon. Fry on all sides until golden brown, then drain on kitchen paper.
- Serve hot.

PREPARATION TIME 2 HOURS
20 MINUTES

COOKING TIME 10 MINUTES

INGREDIENTS

1 tsp yeast
50ml / 1 ¾ fl. oz / ¼ cup water
½ tsp sugar
250g / 9 oz / 1 cup plain (all purpose) flour
1 tsp baking powder
1 tsp black pepper
½ tsp allspice
100ml / 3 ½ fl. oz / ½ cup milk
250g / 9 oz / 1 cup haddock, cooked
1 onion, peeled and finely chopped
2 red chillies, finely chopped
½ Habanero pepper, finely chopped
½ bunch spring onions (scallions), finely chopped
2 tsp dried thyme
1 egg, beaten
Vegetable oil for deep frying

Caribbean Prawn Fritters

362

- Use large langoustines in the batter.

363

SERVES 4

Fish and Sweet Potato Parmentier

PREPARATION TIME 10 MINUTES

COOKING TIME 40-45 MINUTES

....

INGREDIENTS

600g / 1 lb / 2 ½ cups cod fillet, boned
200g / 7 oz / ¾ cup smoked haddock
600ml / 1 pint / 2 ½ cups full-fat milk
1 onion, studded with 2 cloves
2 bay leaves
50g / 1 ¾ oz / ¼ cup butter
50g / 1 ¾ oz / ¼ cup flour
Salt and pepper
½ bunch parsley, finely chopped.
1 kg / 2 ¼ lb / 4 ¼ cups sweet potato, peeled and cut into cubes
2 tbsp Cheddar, grated

- Poach the fish in the milk with the onion and bay leaves for about 8 minutes until just starting to flake. Lift the fish and flavourings out, reserving the milk and leave to cool.
- Heat the butter in a pan and stir in the flour to make a paste. Whisk in the cooking milk a little at a time to make a smooth white sauce.
- Simmer for 15 minutes over a low heat, stirring occasionally. Stir in the parsley and flake in the fish.
- Steam the sweet potato cubes until cooked through – about 10 minutes. Mash thoroughly.
- Preheat the oven to 180°C / 350F / gas 5.
- Spoon the fish in its sauce into individual serving dishes and top with potato. Sprinkle over the cheese and bake for 20-25 minutes until bubbling.

Cod and Potato Parmentier   364

- If you don't like sweet potatoes, this works just as well with floury white potatoes.

365

SERVES 4

Scampi Skewers with Cucumber Salad

PREPARATION TIME 15 MINUTES

COOKING TIME 15 MINUTES

....

INGREDIENTS

100g / 3 ½ oz / 1 ½ cups plain (all purpose) flour
1 egg, beaten
250g / 9 oz / 1 cup fine breadcrumbs
Pinch Cayenne pepper
800g / 1 ¾ lb / 3 ⅓ cups raw scampi
Vegetable oil for deep frying
1 cucumber, halved lengthways and finely sliced
1 bunch dill, chopped
3 tbsp white wine vinegar
½ - 1 tbsp caster (superfine) sugar
1 tsp salt

- Lay the flour, egg and breadcrumbs out in separate dishes, seasoning the breadcrumbs and adding the Cayenne.
- Dip the scampi into each bowl in turn, thoroughly coating each time.
- Heat the oil to 180°C / 350F and cook the scampi in batches until golden brown all over. Drain on kitchen paper.
- Meanwhile macerate the cucumber with the dill and other ingredients to make a light quick pickle.
- Serve with the hot scampi.

Monkfish Skewers   366

- Chunks of meaty monkfish won't fall apart and will provide firm sweetness.

367

SERVES 4

Trout Saltimbocca with Piquillo Peppers

- Sandwich a slice of Serrano ham between 2 trout fillets, skin facing out and secure with toothpicks.
- Dust each side with seasoned flour.
- Heat the butter in a pan until foaming, then lay in 2 trout saltimbocca and cook on each side for 3-4 minutes until golden crusted.
- Keep warm in a low oven while you cook the rest.
- To serve, place the saltimbocca on a plate. Decorate around with the peppers and trout roe and top with a few salad leaves. Serve with lemon wedges on the side.

PREPARATION TIME 10 MINUTES

COOKING TIME 25 MINUTES

INGREDIENTS

8 trout fillets, pin boned
4 slices Serrano ham
2 tbsp flour, seasoned
50g / 1 ¾ oz / ½ cup butter
1 jar piquillo peppers, drained
4 tsp trout roe
1 lemon, quartered
Salad leaves

368

SERVES 4

Steamed Salmon

PREPARATION TIME 5 MINUTES

COOKING TIME 12-16 MINUTES

INGREDIENTS

4 thick salmon steaks
Salt and pepper
4 sprigs thyme or marjoram or chervil

4 tomatoes, thickly sliced
Extra virgin olive oil
½ lemon, juiced

- Set the salmon fillets (probably 2 at a time unless your steamer is industrial) on a plate in a steamer, tucking in the herbs and seasoning.
- Steam over a medium heat for 6-8 minutes, depending on thickness. The inside should be coral pink, not pale pink all the way through otherwise it will be dry.
- Keep the salmon warm while you steam the remaining salmon.
- Meanwhile lay the tomatoes on a plate and drizzle with oil, salt and pepper and lemon juice and leave to macerate.
- Serve the salmon on top of the tomatoes with a squeeze of lemon.

369

SERVES 2

Grilled Sea Bass with Fennel

PREPARATION TIME 10 MINUTES

COOKING TIME 16-18 MINUTES

INGREDIENTS

1 sea bass, gutted and cleaned
1 fennel (finocchio) bulb, trimmed and finely sliced
Few sprigs dill

1 lemon, sliced
Salt and pepper
Olive oil

- Heat a barbecue or griddle until very hot.
- Open up the fish and fill the insides with fennel slices, dill, lemon slices and seasoning.
- Rub the outsides with olive oil and grill for about 8 minutes per side, turning carefully until the fish is just cooked through and pulls away easily from the bone.
- Serve at the table for everyone to help themselves.

370

SERVES 4

Crab Meat Coconut Cakes

PREPARATION TIME 15 MINUTES

COOKING TIME 20 MINUTES

INGREDIENTS

250g / 9 oz / 1 cup white crabmeat, picked
3 tbsp breadcrumbs
1 tbsp unsweetened desiccated coconut
1 egg, beaten
1 clove garlic, crushed
½ red chilli, deseeded and finely chopped
1 tbsp oyster sauce
1 tbsp coriander (cilantro), finely chopped
Salt and pepper
Vegetable oil for deep frying
1 lime, juiced
Lettuce leaves

- Mix together the crab meat, breadcrumbs, egg, garlic, coconut, chilli, oyster sauce and coriander. Season and combine thoroughly.
- Form into small patties of roughly equal size.
- Heat a 1cm depth of oil in a pan and fry the crab cakes in batches until golden brown on both side.
- Drain on kitchen paper and keep warm in a low oven while you cook the rest.
- Serve wrapped in the lettuce leaves sprinkled with lime juice.

Prawn Coconut Cakes 371

- Mince raw prawns in the food processor and proceed as above.

372

SERVES 4

Cod Stew with Wine and Tomato Sauce

PREPARATION TIME 15 MINUTES

COOKING TIME 30 MINUTES

INGREDIENTS

2 tbsp olive oil
1 onion, peeled and finely sliced
1 stick celery, finely chopped
1 carrot, peeled and diced
2 tbsp tomato purée
2 large floury potatoes, peeled and cut into chunks
250ml / 9 fl. oz / 1 cup dry white wine
400ml / 14 fl. oz / 1 ½ cups fish stock
500g / 1 lb / 2 cups cod steak, cut into chunks
1 bouquet garni
2 tbsp parsley, freshly chopped
Salt and pepper

- Heat the oil in a casserole and sweat the onion, celery and carrot until softened.
- Add the tomato puree and cook out for 2 minutes.
- Add the potatoes, then pour over the wine and stock. Add the bouquet garni and fish and bring to a simmer.
- Cook gently for about 20 minutes until the potatoes are tender and the fish is just cooked.
- Season and serve scattered with parsley.

Cod Stew with Red Wine Tomato Sauce 373

- Fish does go well with lighter red wines, so try using one in place of the white wine.

374

SERVES 4 # Marinated Sardines with 3 Pepper Salad

- Place the sardines in a dish with a little oil, rosemary and chilli flakes.
- Mix the peppers in a bowl with the oil, lemon juice and seasoning and leave to macerate.
- Heat a griddle pan until smoking, then cook the sardines for 4-5 minutes each side until cooked through.
- Serve with the crunchy pepper salad and good bread.

PREPARATION TIME 10 MINUTES

COOKING TIME 10 MINUTES

....

INGREDIENTS

12 sardines
Olive oil
Rosemary
Dried chilli flakes
1 red pepper, deseeded and finely chopped
1 yellow pepper, deseeded and finely chopped
1 green pepper, deseeded and finely chopped
2 tbsp extra virgin olive oil
½ lemon, juiced
Salt and pepper

Sardines with Pepper Tomato Salsa

375

- Adding finely chopped tomatoes and a squeeze of lime will make a refreshing accompaniment to the fish.

376

SERVES 3-4 # Herby Fish Cakes

- Combine the fish, potatoes, herbs, capers and a little lemon juice in a bowl and season well.
- Chill for 30 minutes.
- Form into equal-sized patties, then dip into the egg, then the breadcrumbs.
- Heat 1cm depth of oil in a pan and gently fry the fishcakes on both sides until golden and crisp.
- Drain on kitchen paper and serve with peas and ketchup

PREPARATION TIME 40 MINUTES

COOKING TIME 10 MINUTES

....

INGREDIENTS

225g / 8 oz / 1 cup white fish, salmon or tuna, cut into small cubes
225g / 8 oz / 1 cup mashed potato
2 tbsp parsley, chopped
1 tbsp chervil, chopped
3 tsp capers, chopped (optional)
Squeeze of lemon juice
Salt and pepper
1 egg, beaten
3 tbsp breadcrumbs
Vegetable oil

Herby Fish Cakes with a Spicy Crust

377

- A pinch of cayenne with the breadcrumbs will add a kick.

PUDDINGS

378

SERVES 4

Raspberry Fool

- Tip the raspberries into a bowl and lightly crush with a fork so that it is a mixture of liquid and fruit. This will give the fool a more interesting texture.
- Lightly whip the cream to soft peaks, then fold in the yoghurt.
- Fold the raspberries through to make a ripple effect. Taste – you may or may not want the extra sugar.
- Serve in small bowls.

PREPARATION TIME 10 MINUTES

INGREDIENTS

300g / 10 oz / 1 ¼ cups raspberries
150ml / 5 fl. oz / ⅔ cup double cream
125ml / 4 fl. oz / ½ cup Greek natural yoghurt
1 tbsp icing (confectioners') sugar

379

Chocolate and Mint Mousse

SERVES 4

PREPARATION TIME 20 MINUTES

INGREDIENTS

200g / 7oz / ¾ cup dark chocolate
1-2 drops peppermint essence
2 tbsp water
4 eggs, separated
Mint sprigs

- Melt the chocolate and tbsp water in a small bowl over a pan of simmering water.
- Remove the melted chocolate from the heat, leave for 2 minutes, add the peppermint essence, then beat in the egg yolks. Leave to cool for 10 minutes or so.
- Meanwhile whisk the egg whites to soft peaks.
- Fold the egg whites into the chocolate mixture using a metal spoon.
- Spoon into individual glasses or a bowl, cover with clingfilm and chill for at least 6 hours.
- Decorate with mint sprigs.

380

White Chocolate Mousse

SERVES 4

PREPARATION TIME 50 MINUTES

INGREDIENTS

100g / 3 ½ oz / ½ cup good quality white chocolate, broken into pieces
250ml / 9 oz / 1 cup double cream
2 egg whites
1 tbsp caster (superfine) sugar
2 tbsp white chocolate shavings

- Break the chocolate into small pieces and place in a bowl with the cream. Place over a pan of simmering water and whisk until the chocolate has melted. Remove from the heat, leave to cool and then chill for at least 30 minutes.
- Whisk the egg whites, adding the sugar as you whisk, until thick and glossy. Whisk the chocolate mixture until the mixture forms soft peaks, then fold the egg whites in a third at a time, being careful not to lose the air.
- Spoon into individual ramekins and chill until needed.
- Garnish with shavings of white chocolate.

388
SERVES 6
Mascarpone Zabaglione with Strawberries

PREPARATION TIME 3 HOURS

COOKING TIME 35 MINUTES

INGREDIENTS

6 eggs
100g / 3 ½ oz / ½ cup granulated sugar
½ orange, grated zest
100ml / 3 ½ fl. oz / ½ cup dessert or sweet wine
500g / 1 lb / 2 cups mascarpone
24 strawberries
4 tbsp pistachios, shelled and crushed

- Whisk the eggs, sugar and zest with an electric whisk until pale and tripled in volume.
- Tip into a bowl over a pan of simmering water. Very slowly, whisking constantly, pour in the wine, whisking until the eggs have doubled again in volume and the mixture is hot. Take your time as this is when the mixture could curdle.
- Once combined, frothy and voluminous, remove from the heat and whisk for a few more moments to cool.
- Spoon the mascarpone into a bowl and slowly whisk in half the zabaglione. Once combines, fold the remaining half in and spoon into serving glasses.
- Refrigerate for 3 hours before serving. Decorate with strawberries and pistachios.

Mascarpone Zabaglione with Figs 389

- Use quartered figs in place of the strawberries.

390
SERVES 6
Sticky Toffee Pudding

PREPARATION TIME 20 MINUTES

COOKING TIME 40 MINUTES

INGREDIENTS

FOR THE SPONGE
75g / 2 ½ oz / ⅓ cup dates, stoned and finely chopped
1 tsp bicarbonate of soda
50g / 1 ¾ oz / ¼ cup butter
Pinch salt
150g / 5 oz / ⅔ cup Demerara sugar
2 eggs
175g / 6 oz / ¾ cup self raising flour
1 tsp vanilla extract
Butter, softened

FOR THE SAUCE
250ml / 9 fl. oz / 1 cup double cream
80g / 2 ½ oz / ⅓ cup butter
80g / 2 ½ oz / ⅓ cup dark brown sugar

- Preheat the oven to 180°C (160° fan) / 350F / gas 4.
- Pour 275ml / 10 fl. oz / 1 cup boiling water into a bowl and add the dates to soak.
- When the water is lukewarm, add the remaining sponge ingredients, mixing well to combine.
- Pour into a buttered baking dish and bake in the oven for about 40 minutes, or until just firm.
- Heat the sauce ingredients in a pan, whisking regularly.
- When the sponge is cooked, pour over the sauce and flash briefly under a hot grill until bubbling. Serve with ice cream or cream.

Sticky Toffee Pudding with Sherry Cream 391

- To add to the luxury, serve with softly whipped cream folded through with a little sherry.

392
SERVES 4

Summer Fruit Jelly

Autumn Fruit Jelly   393

• Blackberries and late raspberries in a jelly made with a light red beajolais as opposed to rose would make a stunning centrepiece.

Summer Fruit   394
Prosecco Jelly

• Use sparkling prosecco instead of the rose wine.

Peach Jelly   395

• Quartered peaches would work well here too.

PREPARATION TIME 3 HOURS

....

INGREDIENTS

450ml / 1 pint / 2 cups rosé wine
2 tbsp caster (superfine) sugar
3-4 leaves gelatine, soaked in cold water
350g / 12 oz / 1 ½ cups strawberries, hulled and halved
225g / 8 oz / 1 cup raspberries
350g / 12 oz / 1 ½ cups mixed currants, such as blackcurrants, redcurrants, blueberries, blackberries...

• Heat half the wine in a pan, then whisk in the sugar and soaked, squeezed gelatine. Stir to dissolve, then add the remaining wine and pour into a pouring jug to cool.

• Scatter the fruit into the bottom of a large bowl or tureen mould, then pour over the jelly, pushing any fruit down that floats to the surface. Cover with clingfilm and refrigerate for until set.

• To serve, stand the mould in hot water for a few seconds, run a knife around the inside and invert onto a plate.

396

SERVES 4

Apple and Raisin Crumble

PREPARATION TIME 25 MINUTES

COOKING TIME 25-35 MINUTES

....

INGREDIENTS

750g / 1 ⅓ lb / 3 cups apples, peeled,
cored and diced
75g / 2 ½ oz / ⅓ cup raisins, soaked
in a little Calvados or brandy
2 tbsp ground cinnamon

FOR THE CRUMBLE

120g / 4 oz / ½ cup plain
(all purpose) flour
90g 3 oz / ½ cup chilled butter, diced
3 tbsp muscovado sugar
3 tbsp caster (superfine) sugar

• Preheat the oven to 190°C (170° fan) / 370F / gas 5.
• Cook the apples with a little water until soft.
• Put the flour in a bowl with a pinch of salt.
• Add the cold cubes of butter and, using the tips of
  your fingers, work the butter into the flour until the
  mixture resembles porridge oats.
• Place the cooked apple and soaked raisins with the
  cinnamon in the bottom of a baking dish and cover
  loosely with the crumble mixture.
• Cook in the oven for 25-35 minutes until golden
  on top.

Pear Raisin Crumble   397

• Use the same quantity of peeled pears.

398

SERVES 6

Lemon Meringue Pie

PREPARATION TIME I HOUR

COOKING TIME 70 MINUTES

....

INGREDIENTS

125g / 4 oz / ½ cup plain
(all purpose) flour
60g / 2 oz / ¼ cup butter
Pinch salt
Cold water

FOR THE FILLING

3 level tbsp cornflour
60g / 2 oz / ¼ cup caster (superfine)
sugar
300ml / 10 fl. oz / 1 ¼ cups cold
water
Grated zest and juice of 2-3 lemons
2 egg yolks
40g / 1 ½ oz butter

FOR THE MERINGUE

2 egg whites
120g / 4 oz / ½ cup caster (superfine)
sugar

• Preheat the oven to 190°C (170° fan) / 370F / gas 5.
• Make the pastry: Sieve the flour and salt into a large
  bowl, then work the fat into the flour with the pads of
  your fingers until the mixture resembles breadcrumbs.
• Work in 2 tbsp water and bring the mixture together
  with a knife, cutting it through to mix, using enough
  water to just make a smooth ball of dough. Wrap the
  dough in clingfilm and refrigerate.
• Roll the pastry out to just larger than your pie dish.
  Cut a 8mm strip all round, dampen the rim of the dish
  and press the pastry strip on to it. Line the tin with the
  pastry and press the edges onto the pastry rim.
  Prick the base with a fork and bake for 25 minutes.
• Place the cornflour and sugar in a bowl and add
  enough of the water to make a smooth paste. Pour the
  remaining water into a pan with the lemon zest. Bring
  to the boil, pour onto the cornflour paste and mix.
• Tip back into the pan and bring back to the boil for 1
  minute. Remove from the heat and beat in the egg yolks,
  lemon juice and butter. Pour into the pastry shell and
  spread evenly.
• Whisk the egg whites until stiff, then beat in sugar at
  a time until thick and glossy. Spread over the filling,
  sealing the top completely.
• Reduce the oven heat to 150°C / 300F / gas 2 and bake
  for 45 minutes until the meringue is pale gold.

399

SERVES 4 Mississippi Mud Pie

- Stir the crushed biscuits into the melted butter until thoroughly combined, then press into the base of a 23cm pie dish. Chill for 30 minutes.
- Preheat the oven to 180°C (160° fan) / 350F / gas 4.
- Place the chocolate and butter in a bowl over a pan of simmering water and stir until melted. Remove from the heat and leave to cool for 5 minutes.
- Whisk the eggs with the sugar until pale and tripled in volume. Whisk in the melted chocolate in a steady trickle, then whisk in the cocoa powder, cream, vanilla and cayenne if using.
- Pour onto the biscuit base and bake for about 40 minutes until just firm. Leave to cool in the tin and it will sink slightly.
- Serve with softly whipped cream.

Mississippi Mud Pie with Fresh Berries   400

- Serve with raspberries to cut through the chocolate.

PREPARATION TIME 2 HOURS

COOKING TIME 40 MINUTES

INGREDIENTS

75g / 2 ½ oz / ⅓ cup butter, melted
300g / 10 oz / 1 ¼ cups chocolate digestive biscuits

FOR THE FILLING

150g / 5 oz / ⅔ cup dark chocolate, broken up
150g / 5 oz / ⅔ cup butter, cubed
3 eggs
1 tbsp soft brown sugar
1 tbsp cocoa powder
1 tsp vanilla extract
150ml / 5 fl. oz / ⅔ cup double cream
Pinch Cayenne pepper (optional – for a tiny kick)

401

SERVES 4 Poached Pears

- Place the pear peelings and the rest of the poaching ingredients in a large pan and bring to the boil.
- Simmer for 10 minutes to infuse.
- Place the pears upright in the pan and poach gently for around 30 minutes or until completely tender.
- Remove the pears from the liquor and set aside to cool.
- Reduce the poaching liquor by half.
- Serve the pears, with the poaching liquor spooned over.

Poached Pears with Chocolate Sauce   402

- Drizzle some melted dark chocolate over the pears, before serving.

Pears in Red Wine   403

- Red wine works just as well as white with the spices and gives a dramatic colour to the pears.

PREPARATION TIME 10 MINUTES

COOKING TIME 45-50 MINUTES

INGREDIENTS

4 pears, peeled, peelings reserved
500ml / 1 pint / 2 cups white wine
2 tbsp runny honey
75g / 2 ½ oz / ⅓ cup soft brown sugar
Zest of ½ orange + the pared rind of the other half
1 cinnamon stick
1 vanilla pod, split
2 star anise

404
SERVES 4
Chocolate Fondant Puddings

PREPARATION TIME 30 MINUTES

COOKING TIME 8 MINUTES

INGREDIENTS

90g / 3 oz / ⅓ cup caster (superfine) sugar
150g / 5 oz / ⅔ cup butter
150g / 5 oz / ⅔ cup dark chocolate, chopped
3 egg yolks
3 eggs
1 tbsp plain (all purpose) flour
1 tsp vanilla extract

- Preheat the oven to 180°C (160° fan) / 350F / gas 4. Grease 4 individual dariole moulds.
- Place the sugar, butter and chocolate in a bowl set over a pan of simmering water and stir occasionally until melted. Remove from the heat and whisk to combine. Leave to cool for 5 minutes.
- Add the egg yolks and eggs and beat well to combine, then fold in the flour.
- Pour into the moulds and chill for 20 minutes.
- Place on a baking tray and cook for 8 minutes.
- Turn out onto plates and serve immediately.

Chocolate Orange Fondant Puddings
405
- The grated zest of an orange is a classic combo with chocolate.

406
SERVES 4
Eton Mess

PREPARATION TIME 15 MINUTES
+ COOLING TIME

COOKING TIME 1 HOUR

INGREDIENTS

175g / 6 oz / ¾ cup caster (superfine) sugar
3 egg whites
500g / 1 lb / 2 cups raspberries,
1 tbsp icing (confectioners') sugar
500ml / 1 pint / 2 cups double cream
1 tsp vanilla extract

- Preheat the oven to 150°C (130° fan) / 300F / gas 2.
- Whisk the egg whites to soft peaks, then whisk in the sugar a little at a time, beating each addition in thoroughly, until thick and glossy.
- Spoon onto lined baking trays and bake for 1 hour. Turn the oven off and leave until completely cold.
- Purée half the raspberries with the icing sugar until smooth.
- Whisk the cream to soft peaks, whisking in the vanilla as you go.
- Break up the meringues and layer into individual serving dishes, spooning over a little puree, then adding raspberries and cream, swirling the puree in as you go.
- Serve immediately.

Eton Mess with Strawberries
407
- Lightly crush ripe strawberries with a fork for an even more classically British pudding.

Baked Alaska

408 · SERVES 4

- Preheat the oven to its hottest temperature and place a shelf very low down.
- Whisk the egg whites until foamy, then whisk in the salt and cream of tartar until it forms soft peaks. Gradually whisk in the sugar a little at a time until thick and glossy, then fold in the vanilla extract.
- Place the sponge base on a lined baking sheet.
- Using an ice cream scoop, place balls of ice cream on the base, leaving a good edge around the outside.
- Pile the meringue on top, spreading with a palette knife and ensuring the ice cream is completely covered.
- Place under a grill for 2 minutes until golden. Serve immediately.

PREPARATION TIME 20 MINUTES

COOKING TIME 5 MINUTES

INGREDIENTS

6 egg whites
Pinch salt
1 tsp cream of tartar
200g / 7 oz / ¾ cup caster (superfine) sugar
1 tsp vanilla extract
1kg / 2 lb / 4 cups ice cream, slightly softened
1 ready made sponge case

Chocolate Fondant Tart

409 · SERVES 4

PREPARATION TIME 2 HOURS

COOKING TIME 30 MINUTES

INGREDIENTS

3 eggs
300g / 10 oz / 1 ¼ cups muscovado sugar
1 tsp vanilla extract
175g / 6 oz / ¾ cup butter, melted
2 tbsp plain (all purpose) flour
2 tbsp cocoa powder
50g / 1 ¾ oz / ¼ cup dark chocolate, chopped
1 pastry case

FOR THE CUSTARD
300ml / 10 fl. oz / 1 ¼ cups single cream
3 egg yolks
1 tsp cornflour
1 tbsp caster (superfine) sugar
½ tsp vanilla extract

- Preheat the oven to 180°C (160° fan) / 350F / gas 4.
- Beat the eggs and sugar until pale and tripled in volume. Stir in the butter and vanilla, then fold in the flour and cocoa. Scatter the chopped chocolate into the pastry base and pour over the filling.
- Bake for 30 minutes or until just firm. Leave to cool while you make the custard.
- Heat the cream in a pan until nearly boiling. Whisk the egg yolks, cornflour, sugar and vanilla extract.
- Pour the hot cream into the bowl, whisking all the time, then return to the pan. Whisk over a low heat until the sauce has thickened.
- Serve with the chocolate fondant tart.

Baked Apples with Toffee Sauce

410 · SERVES 4

PREPARATION TIME 10 MINUTES

COOKING TIME 20 MINUTES

INGREDIENTS

4 eating apples, cored
2 tbsp butter, softened
1 tsp ground cinnamon
1 orange, grated zest and juice

FOR THE SAUCE
1 vanilla pod, split
250ml / 9 fl. oz / 1 cup double (heavy) cream
80g / 2 ½ oz / ⅓ cup butter
80g / 2 ½ oz / ⅓ cup dark brown sugar

- Preheat the oven to 200°C (180° fan) / 400F / gas 7.
- Score a line around the centre of each apple to help prevent bursting.
- Mix together the butter, cinnamon and orange zest and squeeze in the juice of ½ the orange. Push some of the butter into the centre of each apple.
- Place in a roasting tin, pour a little water into the bottom and dot with any remaining butter mixture. Cover with aluminium foil and bake for 20 minutes or until tender.
- Meanwhile heat the sauce in a pan, stirring until smooth and thickened.
- Pour over the baked apples and serve.

CAKES

Chocolate Coffee Fudge Tart

411

SERVES 4

- Preheat the oven to 180°C / 350F / gas 4.
- Beat the eggs and sugar until pale and tripled in volume. Stir in the butter, coffee and vanilla, then fold in the flour and cocoa. Scatter the chopped chocolate into the pastry base and pour over the filling.
- Bake for 30 minutes or until just firm. Leave to cool.
- Decorate with coffee beans.

PREPARATION TIME 30-40 MINUTES + CHILLING TIME

COOKING TIME 30 MINUTES

INGREDIENTS

3 eggs
300g / 10 oz / 1 ¼ cups muscovado sugar
1 tsp vanilla extract
30ml / 1 fl. oz espresso coffee
175g / 6 oz / ¾ cup butter, melted
2 tbsp plain (all purpose) flour
2 tbsp cocoa powder
50g / 1 ¾ oz / ¼ cup dark (bittersweet) chocolate, chopped
1 pastry case
Coffee beans

Victoria Sponge

412

SERVES 6-8

PREPARATION TIME 40 MINUTES

COOKING TIME 25 MINUTES

INGREDIENTS

120g / 4 oz / ½ cup butter, at room temperature
120g / 4 oz / ½ cup caster (superfine) sugar
2 eggs
1 tsp vanilla extract
120g / 4 oz / ½ cup self raising flour
Raspberry or strawberry jam (jelly)
Icing (confectioners') sugar

- Preheat the oven to 170°C / 325F / gas 3. Grease and line 2 x 18cm / 7in sponge tins.
- Cream the butter and sugar together until pale and creamy.
- Whisk the eggs thoroughly, then beat into the butter mixture a little at a time until fully incorporated.
- Stir in the vanilla extract, then sieve the flour a little at a time into the bowl and fold in with a metal spoon. If the batter is a little thick, add a little hot water to loosen.
- Spoon into the tins, then bake for 25 minutes or until springy and golden.
- Leave to cool for 10 minutes. Remove from the tins and cool on a wire rack. Sandwich with the jam and dust with icing sugar to serve.

Lemon Drizzle Cake

413

SERVES 6

PREPARATION TIME 25 MINUTES

COOKING TIME 40-45 MINUTES

INGREDIENTS

120g / 4 oz / ½ cup butter, softened
175g / 6 oz / ¾ cup caster (superfine) sugar
2 eggs
1 lemon, grated zest
175g / 6 oz / ¾ cup self raising flour
100ml / 3 ½ fl. oz / ½ cup milk

FOR THE SYRUP
2 lemons, juiced
100g / 3 ½ oz / ½ cup icing (confectioners') sugar

FOR THE GLAZE
½ lemon, juiced
150g / 5 oz / ⅔ cup icing (confectioners') sugar

- Preheat the oven to 180°C / 350F / gas 4. Grease and line a loaf tin.
- Cream the butter and sugar until pale and creamy, then whisk in the eggs a little at a time.
- Whisk in the zest, then, using a metal spoon, fold in the flour, salt and then stir in the milk. Spoon into the loaf tin and bake for 40-45 minutes until a skewer comes out clean when poked into the centre. Set aside.
- Heat the lemon juice and sugar in a pan until the sugar dissolves. Puncture the surface of the cake with a skewer and pour over the hot syrup. Leave to cool completely then remove from the tin.
- Whisk together the lemon juice and sugar to make the glaze, then drizzle over the top of the cake.

414
SERVES 8-10 Chocolate Fudge Cake

PREPARATION TIME 30 MINUTES

COOKING TIME 30 MINUTES

INGREDIENTS

120g / 4 oz / ½ cup self raising flour
1 tsp baking powder
120g / 4 oz / ½ cup butter, softened
120g / 4 oz / ½ cup caster (superfine) sugar
2 eggs
1 ½ tbsp cocoa powder

FOR THE FILLING AND ICING
75g / 2 ½ oz / ⅓ cup granulated sugar
75ml / 2 ½ oz / ⅓ cup evaporated milk
120g / 4 oz / ½ cup dark chocolate, chopped
40g / 1 oz butter, softened
25g / 1 oz chocolate, shaved

- Preheat the oven to 170°C (150° fan) / 325F / gas 3. Grease and line 2 x 18cm / 7 in cake tins.
- Sieve the flour and baking powder into a large bowl, then add the other ingredients.
- Divide the mixture equally between the two cake tins and cook for 30 minutes.
- Remove from the tins and cool on a wire rack.
- Make the icing: Combine the sugar and evaporated milk in a pan and stir to dissolve the sugar.
- Bring to the boil and simmer for 5 minutes, then stir in the chocolate and butter. Chill for at least 1 hour until it has thickened and is spreadable.
- Use the icing to sandwich the cakes together, then smooth the remainder over the top and sides with a palette knife. Decorate with chocolate shavings.

Chocolate Fudge Cake with Raspberry Filling | 415
- Spread a thick layer of good quality raspberry or even cherry preserve on the sponge.

416
SERVES 4 Carrot Cake

PREPARATION TIME 20 MINUTES

COOKING TIME 1 HOUR 30 MINUTES

INGREDIENTS

300g / 10 oz / 1 ¼ cups plain (all purpose) flour
1 tsp ground cinnamon
1 tsp baking powder
½ tsp bicarbonate of soda
200g / 7 oz / ¾ cup soft dark brown sugar
4 eggs
250ml / 9 fl. oz / 1 cup vegetable oil
Zest of 2 oranges
200g / 7 oz / ¾ cup carrots, peeled and grated
125g / 4 oz / ½ cup butter, softened
2 tbsp icing (confectioners') sugar
250g / 9 oz / 1 cup cream cheese
Zest of ½ lemon

- Preheat the oven to 150°C (130° fan) / 300F / gas 2. Grease and line a 20cm cake tin.
- Sieve the flour into a bowl with cinnamon, baking powder and bicarbonate of soda, then stir in the sugar.
- Beat the eggs with the oil and fold into the flour with the carrots and orange zest.
- Spoon into the cake tin and bake for about 1 ½ hours until an inserted skewer comes out clean. Leave to cool.
- Beat the butter and sugar together until pale, then beat in the cream cheese and lemon zest. Chill until spreadable and cover the cake using a palette knife to smooth.

Spiced Carrot Cake | 417
- A pinch of mixed spice with the cinnamon will add flavour.

418

SERVES 8-10

Coffee Cinnamon Cake

Coffee Cake with Crushed Walnuts

419

- Lightly pulse walnuts in a blender and sprinkle over the top.

Coffee Cake with Caramelised Pecans

420

- Chop pecan nuts and coat in a light caramel before arranging on the cake.

Coffee Cake with Cinnamon Sugar

421

- Mix together brown sugar and cinnamon and sprinkle over the cake.

PREPARATION TIME 30 MINUTES

COOKING TIME 30 MINUTES

INGREDIENTS

120g / 4 oz / ½ cup self raising flour
1 tsp baking powder
120g / 4 oz / ½ cup butter, softened
120g / 4 oz / ½ cup caster (superfine) sugar
90 g / 3 oz / ½ cup mixed nuts, chopped
2 eggs
1 tbsp coffee mixed with 1 tbsp hot water
1 tsp ground cinnamon

FOR THE FILLING AND ICING
225g / 8 oz / 1 cup icing (confectioners') sugar
100g / 3 ½ oz / ½ cup butter, softened
2 tbsp instant coffee dissolved in
1 tbsp hot water
¼ tsp ground cinnamon

- Preheat the oven to 170°C (150° fan) / 325F / gas 3. Grease and line 2 x 18cm / 7 in cake tins.
- Sieve the flour and baking powder into a large bowl, then add the other ingredients and whisk until completely combined.
- Divide the mixture equally between the two cake tins and top with the nuts, cook for 30 minutes.
- Remove from the tins and cool on a wire rack.
- Make the icing: Cream the butter and sugar together, then stir in the coffee. Refrigerate until needed.
- Use the icing to sandwich the cakes together, then smooth the remainder over the top and sides with a palette knife. Dust with a little cinnamon

422

SERVES 8-10 # Chocolate Cake with Buttercream Filling

Chocolate Cake with Citrus Buttercream 423

- Add the grated zest of 1 orange to the buttercream and a squeeze of the juice.

Chocolate Cake with Jam and Buttercream 424

- Double the pleasure by adding a thick layer of strawberry jam.

Chocolate Cake with Chocolate Buttercream 425

- .Sift in 1 tbsp cocoa powder to the filling and fold in.

PREPARATION TIME 30 MINUTES

COOKING TIME 30 MINUTES

INGREDIENTS

120g / 4 oz / ½ cup self raising flour
1 tsp baking powder
120g / 4 oz / ½ cup butter, softened
120g / 4 oz / ½ cup caster (superfine) sugar
2 eggs
1 ½ tbsp cocoa powder

FOR THE FILLING
100g / 3 ½ oz / ½ cup butter, softened
150g / 5 oz / ⅔ cup icing (confectioners') sugar
1 tsp vanilla extract

- Preheat the oven to 170°C (150° fan) / 325F / gas 3. Grease and line 2 x 18cm / 7 in cake tins.
- Sieve the flour and baking powder into a large bowl, then add the other ingredients and whisk until completely combined.
- Divide the mixture equally between the two cake tins and cook for 30 minutes.
- Remove from the tins and cool on a wire rack.
- Make the icing: Cream the butter and sugar until pale and smooth, then stir in the vanilla.
- Use the icing to sandwich the cakes together.
- Decorate with a little caster sugar.

426

SERVES 4

Black Forest Gateau

- Preheat the oven to 190°C (170° fan) / 375F / gas 5. Grease and line 2 x 20cm / 8in sandwich tins.
- Mix the butter, sugar, flour, cocoa powder, baking powder and eggs in a food processor until smooth.
- Divide equally between the bake tins and bake for 25 minutes until risen. Turn onto a wire rack. Leave to cool completely. Slice the cakes in half horizontally.
- Heat the jam with the cherries and Kirsch for 5 minutes. Leave to cool. Spread over three of the sponges. Whisk 300ml / 10 fl. oz of the cream to soft peaks.
- Transfer a cherry-topped sponge to a plate, then smooth on ⅓ of the cream. Sprinkle with chocolate.
- Top with a cherry-topped sponge and repeat, then with the third sponge. Place the final clean sponge on top.
- Whisk the cream to soft peaks. Smooth over the cake top and sides with a palette knife. Finish with grated chocolate.

Black Forest Gateau with Chocolate Curls

427

- Shave chocolate with a peeler to make chocolate curls and a more elaboate decoration.

PREPARATION TIME I HOUR

COOKING TIME 25 MINUTES

....

INGREDIENTS

250g / 9 oz / 1 cup butter, softened
250g / 9 oz / 1 cup caster (superfine) sugar
150g / 5 oz / ⅔ cup self raising flour
3 tbsp cocoa powder
1 tsp baking powder
4 eggs
350g / 12 oz / 1 ½ cups morello cherry jam (jelly)
1 jar or can bottled cherries and their juice
3 tbsp Kirsch
500ml / 1 pint / 2 cups double cream
50g / 1 ¾ oz / ¼ cup dark chocolate, grated

428

SERVES 8

Battenberg Cake

- Preheat the oven to 190°C (170° fan) / 375F / gas 5. Grease and line a 20cm / 8in square cake tin.
- Cut a piece of baking parchment 30x20cm and make an 8cm fold in the centre. Place in the tin with the fold in the centre.
- Mix the butter, sugar, eggs, flour and vanilla in a food processor. Weigh out half the batter and place the two amounts in separate bowls. Add red food dye to one.
- Spoon the batters into each half of the sponge tin. Bake for 30 minutes. Cool for 5 minutes, then place on a wire rack.
- Place one sponge on top of the other and trim off any overhanging edges so they are exactly the same size. Cut in half lengthways to make 4 long rectangles.
- Brush the long side of one of the plain sponges with jam and press against a pink sponge. Repeat with the other two sponges.
- Sandwich the two pairs of sponges to make a checker board pattern, then brush all over with apricot jam.
- Dust the surface with icing sugar and roll out the marzipan to 5mm thick and large enough to completely encase the sponges. Wrap the marzipan around the cake, pressing the edges together to make a firm join.
- Turn seam side down, trim a thin slice off each end and serve.

PREPARATION TIME 45 MINUTES

COOKING TIME 30 MINUTES

....

INGREDIENTS

175g / 6 oz / ¾ cup butter, softened
175g / 6 oz / ¾ cup caster (superfine) sugar
3 eggs
175g / 6 oz / ¾ cup self raising flour
1 tsp vanilla extract
Red food dye
6-8 tbsp apricot jam (jelly), warmed
500g / 1lb ready rolled marzipan
Icing (confectioners') sugar

Banana Loaf Cake

429 · SERVES 4

PREPARATION TIME 20 MINUTES

COOKING TIME 1-1 HOUR 30 MINUTES

INGREDIENTS

350g / 12 oz over ripe bananas
180g / 6 oz / ¾ cup plain (all purpose) flour
2 tsp baking powder
1 tsp ground cinnamon
¼ tsp mixed spice
Pinch salt
150g / 5 oz / ⅔ cup soft dark brown sugar
2 eggs, beaten
100g / 3 ½ oz / ¼ cup butter, melted

- Preheat the oven to 170°C (150° fan) / 325F / gas 3. Grease a medium loaf tin.
- Mash the bananas in a bowl until pulpy.
- Sieve the flour into a bowl with the baking powder, spices and salt.
- Whisk the sugar and eggs until pale and creamy and doubled in volume, then whisk in the butter. Fold in the bananas and flour until thoroughly combined.
- Pour into the loaf tin and bake for 1 -1 ½ hours or until an inserted skewer comes out clean.
- Turn onto a wire rack to cool.

Banana Apple Loaf Cake · 430

- Add ½ grated apple and 1 tbsp rum to the mix.

Raisin Cake

431 · SERVES 6

PREPARATION TIME 20 MINUTES

COOKING TIME 1-1 ½ HOURS

INGREDIENTS

175g / 6 oz / ¾ cup soft light brown sugar
175g / 6 oz / ¾ cup butter, softened
3 eggs, beaten
275g / 10 oz / 1 heaped cup self raising flour
2 tsp mixed spice
175g / 6 oz / ¾ cup raisins, soaked in a little brandy
3 tbsp milk

- Preheat the oven to 180°C (160° fan) / 350F / gas 5.
- Cream the butter and sugar until pale and creamy. Add the eggs a little at a time, beating thoroughly after each addition, until well combined. Fold in the flour, spice and raisins. Add a little milk to loosen the batter.
- Spoon into a loaf tin and bake for 1-1 ½ hours until risen and springy or until an inserted skewer comes out clean.
- Turn onto a wire rack and leave to cool.

Chocolate and Raisin Cake · 432

- Add 175 g / 6 oz of chocolate chips to the batter before baking.

Golden Raisin Cake · 433

- Golden raisins mixed with ordinary ones make a glorious colour.

Coconut Cake

434

SERVES 8

Coconut Rum Cake
435
- Whisk 2 tbsp white rum into the icing for a boozy hit.

Coconut Cake with Orange Icing
436
- Stir in grated zest of 1 orange into the icing.

Coconut Cake with Dark Chocolate
437
- Grate over dark chocolate for the 'Bounty' effect.

PREPARATION TIME 30 MINUTES

COOKING TIME 40 MINUTES

INGREDIENTS

200g / 7 oz / ¾ cup plain (all purpose) flour
Pinch salt
2 tsp baking powder
75g / 2 ½ oz / ⅓ cup butter, chilled and cubed
75g / 2 ½ oz / ⅓ cup caster (superfine) sugar
50g / 1 ¾ oz / ¼ cup desiccated coconut
1 lime, grated zest
1 egg
120ml / 4 fl. oz / ½ cup milk
1 tsp vanilla extract

FOR THE ICING

100g / 3 ½ oz / ½ cup butter, softened
150g / 5 oz / ⅔ cup icing (confectioners') sugar
1 tsp vanilla extract
Desiccated coconut to decorate

- Preheat the oven to 180°C (160° fan) / 350F / gas 5. Grease and line a cake tin.
- Sieve the flour, salt, baking powder into a bowl. Using the pads of your fingertips, rub the butter in until it resembles breadcrumbs. Stir in the sugar, coconut and lime zest.
- Whisk the egg and milk together with the vanilla. Make a well in the flour mixture, then add the liquid a little at a time to for a smooth batter.
- Spoon into the cake tin and bake for about 40 minutes, or until an inserted skewer comes out clean. Cool on a wire rack.
- Cream the butter and sugar together until pale and creamy, then whisk in the vanilla. Spread over the cake with a palette knife and decorate with desiccated coconut and grated lime zest.

438

SERVES 4

Madeira Cake

Madeira with Warm Poached Fruit

439

- Gently cook berries in a little water and sugar to serve with the cake.

Madeira with Whipped Cream

440

- Softly whip some cream with a little grand marnier to serve with the warmed cake.

Madeira with Chocolate Sauce

441

- Melt dark chocolate with enough cream to make a rich thick sauce to dip fingers of the cake in.

PREPARATION TIME 20 MINUTES

COOKING TIME 40 MINUTES

INGREDIENTS

175g / 6 oz / ¾ cup butter, at room temperature
175g / 6 oz / ¾ cup caster (superfine) sugar
3 eggs, beaten
250g / 9 oz / 1 cup self raising flour
3 tbsp milk
½ lemon, grated zest
½ orange, grated zest

- Preheat oven to 180°C (160° fan) / 350F / gas 4. Grease and line a loaf tin.
- Cream the butter and sugar until pale and creamy, then beat in the eggs, a little at a time, beating each addition in thoroughly.
- Sieve the flour into the bowl and fold in with a metal spoon along with the milk to make a loose batter. Fold in the citrus zest.
- Spoon into the loaf tin and bake for 40 minutes or until golden brown and an inserted skewer comes out clean.
- Leave to cool for 5 minutes, then transfer to a wire rack and leave to cool completely.

442
SERVES 8

Marble Cake

- Preheat the oven to 180°C (160° fan) / 350F / gas 4. Grease and line a 20cm cake tin.
- Cream the butter and sugar together until pale and creamy. Add the eggs a little at a time, whisking to combine each addition thoroughly.
- Using a metal spoon fold in the flour gently, then add the milk and vanilla extract and combine well.
- Divide the mixture equally between 2 bowls and sieve the cocoa powder into one. Using 2 large spoons, place dollops of the mixtures alternately into the cake tin, then swirl around with a skewer to marble the mixture.
- Bake in the oven for 50-60 minutes until a skewer comes out clean.
- Turn onto a cooling rack and leave to cool.

Marble Cake with Poached Strawberries
443

- Cook strawberries in a little orange juice and black pepper to serve alongside.

PREPARATION TIME 30 MINUTES

COOKING TIME 50-60 MINUTES

INGREDIENTS

225g / 9 oz / 1 cup butter, softened
225g / 9 oz / 1 cup caster (superfine) sugar
4 eggs, beaten
225g / 9 oz / 1 cup self raising flour
3 tbsp milk
1 tsp vanilla extract
2 tbsp cocoa powder

444
SERVES 6-8

Christmas Cake

- Soak all the fruit in the brandy in a bowl overnight.
- The next day preheat the oven to 150°C / 300F / gas 2. Grease and line a 23 cm springform cake tin.
- Cream the butter and sugar, then beat in the zest. Add the eggs a little at a time then add the almond essence.
- Fold in the flour, spices and the soaked fruit.
- Pour into the cake tin and bake for about 3 hours, until an inserted skewer comes out clean.
- Remove from the tin, wrap in foil and store in an airtight container for at least 3 weeks. You could feed the cake with a tbsp brandy every other day.
- Warm the jam in a small pan and paint over the cake. Roll out the marzipan and press onto the cake, cutting away the excess and smoothing away any air bubbles.
- Roll out the icing and cover the cake with it, cutting away any excess. Decorate as desired.

Christmas Cake with Cheese
445

- Serve alongside a wedge of Wensleydale cheese as per the Yorkshire tradition.

PREPARATION TIME 25 MINUTES

COOKING TIME 3 HOURS

INGREDIENTS

700g / 1 ⅓ lb / 3 cups sultanas
225g / 8 oz / 1 cup raisins
110g / 4 oz / ½ cup currants
110g / 4 oz / ½ cup glaće cherries
110g / 4 oz / ½ cup mixed peel
120ml / 4 fl. oz / ½ cup brandy
225g / 8 oz / 1 cup butter, softened
200g / 7 oz / ¾ cup brown sugar
1 lemon, grated zest
1 orange, grated zest
4 eggs, beaten
1 tsp almond essence
350g / 12 oz / 1 ½ cups plain (all purpose) flour
1 tsp mixed spice
½ tsp ground cinnamon
Pinch salt
200g / 7 oz / ¾ cup apricot jam (jelly)
500g / 1 lb marzipan
1kg / 2 lb ready to roll icing (frosting)

SWEET TREATS

Blueberry Muffins

446 · MAKES 12

- Preheat the oven to 200°C (180° fan) / 400F / gas 6. Line a 12 hole muffin tin.
- In a bowl, whisk together the sugar, oil, egg and buttermilk.
- Stir through the blueberries, then sieve in the flour with the baking powder and bicarbonate. Fold until lightly blended, but still a little lumpy. This will help keep the muffins light.
- Spoon evenly into the muffin cases then bake for about 25 minutes or until golden and risen.

PREPARATION TIME 15 MINUTES

COOKING TIME 25 MINUTES

INGREDIENTS

250g / 9 oz / 1 cup caster (superfine) sugar
80ml / 2 ½ fl. oz / ⅓ cup vegetable oil
1 egg
250ml / 9 fl. oz / 1 cup buttermilk
200g / 7 oz / ⅔ cup blueberries
300g / 10 oz / 1 ¼ cups plain (all purpose) flour
2 tsp baking powder
1 tsp bicarbonate of soda

Chocolate Chip Muffins

447 · MAKES 12

PREPARATION TIME 15 MINUTES

COOKING TIME 25 MINUTES

INGREDIENTS

250g / 9 oz / 1 cup caster (superfine) sugar
80ml / 2 ½ fl. oz / ⅓ cup vegetable oil
1 egg
250ml / 9 fl. oz / 1 cup buttermilk
200g / 7 oz / ⅔ cup dark chocolate chips
300g / 10 oz / 1 ¼ cups plain (all purpose) flour
2 tsp baking powder
1 tsp bicarbonate of soda

- Preheat the oven to 200°C (180° fan) / 400F / gas 6. Line a 12 hole muffin tin.
- In a bowl, whisk together the sugar, oil, egg and buttermilk.
- Stir through the chocolate chips, then sieve in the flour with the baking powder and bicarbonate. Fold until lightly blended, but still a little lumpy. This will help keep the muffins light.
- Spoon evenly into the muffin cases then bake for about 25 minutes or until golden and risen.

Walnut Brownies

448 · MAKES 16

PREPARATION TIME 15 MINUTES

COOKING TIME 30 MINUTES

INGREDIENTS

120g / 4 oz / ½ cup butter
50g / 2 oz / ¼ cup dark chocolate
2 eggs, beaten
225g / 8 oz / 1 cup granulated sugar
50g / 2 oz / ½ cup plain (all purpose) flour
1 tsp baking powder
Pinch salt
150g / 5 oz / ⅔ cup walnuts, chopped

- Preheat the oven to 180°C (160° fan) / 350F / gas 4.
- Melt the butter and chocolate in a bowl over a pan of simmering water.
- Once melted, stir in the other ingredients until smooth and combined.
- Pour into a tin and bake for 30 minutes until the centre feels springy to the touch.
- Leave to cool in the tin before dividing into 16 squares and cooling on a wire rack.

449
MAKES 12

Lemon Cupcakes

PREPARATION TIME 20 MINUTES

COOKING TIME 20 MINUTES

INGREDIENTS

120g / 4 oz / ½ cup self raising flour
120g / 4 oz / ½ cup caster (superfine) sugar
120g / 4 oz / ½ cup butter, softened
2 eggs, beaten
1 lemon, grated zest
2 tbsp milk

FOR THE TOPPING
120g / 4 oz / ½ cup butter, softened
250g / 9 oz / 1 cup icing (confectioners') sugar
1 lemon, juice

- Preheat the oven to 200°C (180° fan) / 400F / gas 6. Line a 12 hole muffin tin with cases.
- Place all the cupcake ingredients except the milk in a food processor and blitz until smooth and combined.
- Add the milk a little at a time to make a dropping consistency.
- Divide the mixture evenly between the cases and bake for 20 minutes or until risen and golden.
- Meanwhile cream the butter with the icing sugar until pale and creamy, then stir in the lemon juice.
- Remove the cakes from the tin to a wire rack to cool then decorate with the lemon icing.

Lime Cupcakes
450

- Use lime in place of the lemon – you may need an extra one.

451
MAKES 12

Chocolate Cupcakes

PREPARATION TIME 25 MINUTES

COOKING TIME 20 MINUTES

INGREDIENTS

120g / 4 oz / ½ cup self raising flour
120g / 4 oz / ½ cup caster (superfine) sugar
120g / 4 oz / ½ cup butter, softened
2 eggs, beaten
1 tbsp cocoa powder
2 tbsp milk

FOR THE TOPPING
90g / 3 ½ oz / white chocolate, chopped
350g / 12 oz / / 1 ½ cups butter, softened
300g / 10 ½ oz / 1 ¼ cups icing (confectioners') sugar
120ml / 4 fl. oz / ½ cup double cream
Chocolate buttons, for decorating

- Preheat the oven to 200°C (180° fan) / 400F / gas 6. Line a 12 hole muffin tin with cases.
- Place all the cupcake ingredients except the milk in a food processor and blitz until smooth and combined. Add the milk a little at a time to make a dropping consistency.
- Divide the mixture evenly between the cases and bake for 20 minutes or until risen and golden.
- Meanwhile place the chocolate in a bowl set over a pan of simmering water and stir until melted. Set aside to cool slightly.
- Whisk the butter, icing sugar until pale, then whisk in the melted chocolate. Whisk in the cream until smooth and lightened.
- Remove the cakes from the tin to a wire rack to cool then decorate with the icing and chocolate buttons.

Chocolate Cupcakes with Chocolate Buttons
452

- Decorate with good quality chocolate buttons and spray silver if desired.

Almond Chocolate Chip Brownies

(453)

MAKES 16

Almond Brownies with Cherries

(454)

- Stir in 2 tbsp chopped glace cherries for extra chew.

Pecan Chocolate Brownies

(455)

- Use pecan nuts in place of the almonds.

Almond Double Chocolate Chip Brownies

(456)

- Try adding a handful of white chocolate chips to the mix to melt as it cooks.

PREPARATION TIME 15 MINUTES

COOKING TIME 30 MINUTES

....

INGREDIENTS

120g / 4 oz / ½ cup butter
50g / 2 oz / ¼ cup dark chocolate
2 eggs, beaten
225g / 8 oz / 1 cup granulated sugar
50g / 2 oz / ½ cup plain (all purpose) flour
1 tsp baking powder
Pinch salt
120g / 4 oz / ½ cup almonds, chopped
120g / 4 oz / ½ cup dark or white chocolate chips

- Preheat the oven to 180°C (160° fan) / 350F / gas 4.
- Melt the butter and chocolate in a bowl over a pan of simmering water.
- Once melted, stir in the other ingredients apart from the chocolate chips until smooth and combined.
- Tip in the chocolate chips and stir to distribute then pour into a tin and bake for 30 minutes until the centre feels springy to the touch.
- Leave to cool in the tin before dividing into 16 squares and cooling on a wire rack.

457
MAKES 12-16 # Chocolate Chip Cookies

Double Chocolate Cookies
458

- Add a handful of white chocolate chips as well as the dark.

Cranberry Chocolate Cookies
459

- Use chopped dried cranberries in place of the chocolate chips.

Nutty Chocolate Cookies
460

- Use chopped hazelnuts in place of the chocolate chips.

PREPARATION TIME 20-30 MINUTES

COOKING TIME 20 MINUTES

INGREDIENTS

120g / 4 oz / ½ cup dark chocolate, chopped
150g / 5 oz / ⅔ cup plain (all purpose) flour
1 tbsp cocoa powder
1 tsp bicarbonate of soda
Pinch salt
120g / 4 oz / ½ cup butter, softened
120g / 4 oz / ½ cup caster (superfine) sugar
1 egg
350g / 12 oz / 1 ½ cups chocolate chips, white or dark

- Preheat the oven to 170°C (150° fan) / 325F / gas 3.
- Place the chocolate in a bowl over a pan over simmering water and stir until melted. Set aside to cool.
- Tip the flour, cocoa powder and bicarbonate into a bowl and stir in the salt.
- Cream the butter and sugar in a bowl until pale and creamy, then whisk in the melted chocolate.
- Whisk in the egg, then the dry ingredients, then the chocolate chips.
- Splodge fairly even amounts onto a lined baking sheet about 6cm apart. Cook for 20 minutes or until an inserted skewer comes out not wet with batter – it won't be clean.
- Leave to cool then transfer to a wire rack. Best eaten warm and soft.

461
MAKES 12 Vanilla Cupcakes

- Preheat the oven to 200°C (180° fan) / 400F / gas 6. Line a 12 hole muffin tin with cases.
- Place all the ingredients except the milk in a food processor and blitz until smooth and combined.
- Add the milk a little at a time to make a dropping consistency.
- Divide the mixture evenly between the cases and bake for 20 minutes or until risen and golden.
- Remove the cakes from the tin to a wire rack to cool.

PREPARATION TIME 20 MINUTES

COOKING TIME 20 MINUTES

INGREDIENTS

120g / 4 oz / ½ cup self raising flour
120g / 4 oz / ½ cup caster (superfine) sugar
120g / 4 oz / ½ cup butter, softened
2 eggs, beaten
1 tsp vanilla extract
2 tbsp milk

Buttercream Cupcakes 462

- Decorate with mixed candied peel and a flavoured buttercream.

463
MAKES 24 Shortbread Biscuits

- Preheat the oven to 190°C (170° fan) / 375F / gas 5.
- Cream the butter and sugar until pale and creamy.
- Whisk in the flour a little at a time until thoroughly incorporated. Turn the dough out onto a floured surface and roll out to 1cm thickness.
- Cut out equal sized rounds or fingers and place on a baking tray. Refrigerate for 20 minutes.
- Bake in the oven for about 20 minutes or until pale gold. Set aside to cool on a wire rack, then dust with sugar.

PREPARATION TIME 15 MINUTES

COOKING TIME 20 MINUTES

INGREDIENTS

120g / 4 oz / ½ cup butter, softened
60g / 2 oz / ¼ cup caster (superfine) sugar
180g / 6 oz / ¾ cup plain (all purpose) flour
1 tsp vanilla extract (optional)
Sugar, for dusting

Shortbread Biscuits with Poached Fruit 464

- Gently warm berries in a little water and sugar for an instant dessert.

465

MAKES 12

Hot Cross Buns

PREPARATION TIME I HOUR
45 MINUTES

COOKING TIME 15 MINUTES

INGREDIENTS

500g / 1 lb / 2 cups strong white
bread flour
75g / 2 ½ oz / ⅓ cup butter
3 tbsp caster (superfine) sugar
1 tsp salt
1 tsp ground cinnamon
½ tsp ground mixed spice
¼ tsp grated nutmeg
1 ½ tsp fast action dried yeast
1 egg, beaten
275ml / 9 ½ fl. oz / 1 scant cup milk
120g / 4 oz / ½ cup golden sultanas

TO DECORATE

120g / 4 oz / ½ cup plain (all
purpose) four
8 tbsp water
4 tbsp milk
2 tbsp sugar

- Place the flour in a large bowl and rub in the butter using the pads of your fingertips until the mixture resembles breadcrumbs.
- Stir in the sugar, salt, spices and yeast, whisk in the egg and then gradually add the milk.
- Knead on a floured surface for 5 minutes until the dough is smooth and elastic. Work in the sultanas, then return to the bowl, cover with clingfilm and leave in a warm place to rise for 1 hour or until doubled in size.
- Tip the dough out onto the surface and knead well for 5 minutes. Cut into 12 equal pieces, then shape each one into a smooth ball, tucking any joins or seams underneath. Place, spaced well apart, on a greased baking sheet. Cover again with oiled clingfilm and leave in a warm place for 30 minutes.
- Preheat the oven to 200°C / 400F / gas 6.
- To make the crosses, sieve the flour into a small bowl and mix in the water to make a smooth paste. Pipe crosses onto the buns.
- Bake in the oven for about 15 minutes.
- Meanwhile place the milk and sugar in a pan and heat until the sugar has dissolved and the liquid is syrupy. Brush over the baked buns, transfer to a wire rack and cool.

466

MAKES 30-40

Butter Cookies

PREPARATION TIME I HOUR
20 MINUTES

COOKING TIME 15 MINUTES

INGREDIENTS

370g / 13 oz / 1 ½ cups plain (all
purpose) flour
Pinch salt
250g / 9 oz / 1 cup butter, softened
1 egg yolk
120g / 4 oz / ½ cup caster (superfine)
sugar
1 tsp vanilla extract
Or 1 lemon, grated zest

- Sieve the flour and salt into a bowl. Set aside.
- Cream the butter and sugar until pale and creamy. Whisk in the egg yolk and flavouring, then work in the flour a little at a time.
- Bring the dough together into a ball, wrap in clingfilm and refrigerate for 1 hour.
- Preheat the oven to 180°C (160° fan) / 350F / gas 4.
- Roll the dough out on a floured surface to about 3mm thickness. Cut out with your preferred cookie cutter shapes, or simply stamp out circles and place on lined baking sheets.
- Bake for about 15 minutes until pale gold. Transfer to a wire rack to cool.

Citrus Butter Cookies

467

- Add the zest of ½ orange as well as the lemon.

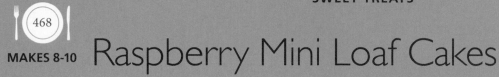

MAKES 8-10 # Raspberry Mini Loaf Cakes

Cherry Loaf Cake 469

- Use stoned cherries in place of the raspberries.

Strawberry Loaf Cake 470

- Use hulled halved strawberries.

Blackberry Loaf Cake 471

- Use blackberries in place of the raspberries.

PREPARATION TIME 20 MINUTES

COOKING TIME 20 MINUTES

INGREDIENTS

120g / 4 oz / ½ cup self raising flour
120g / 4 oz / ½ cup caster (superfine) sugar
120g / 4 oz / ½ cup butter, softened
2 eggs, beaten
1 tsp vanilla extract
2 tbsp milk
1 punnet raspberries

- Preheat the oven to 200°C (180° fan) / 400F / gas 6. Line individual mini-loaf cake tins or simply line a muffin tin with cases if you don't have any.
- Place all the ingredients except the milk in a food processor and blitz until smooth and combined.
- Add the milk a little at a time to make a dropping consistency.
- Divide the mixture evenly between the cases and push 3-4 raspberries down the middle of each loaf cake. Bake for 20 minutes or until risen and golden.
- Remove the cakes from the tin to a wire rack to cool.

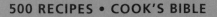

472

MAKES 12

Lemon Meringue Cupcakes

PREPARATION TIME 30 MINUTES

COOKING TIME 20 MINUTES

....

INGREDIENTS

120g / 4 oz / ½ cup self raising flour
120g / 4 oz / ½ cup caster (superfine) sugar
120g / 4 oz / ½ cup butter, softened
2 eggs, beaten
1 lemon, grated zest
2 tbsp milk

FOR THE TOPPING
2 egg whites
120g / 4 oz / ½ cup caster (superfine) sugar

- Preheat the oven to 200°C (180° fan) / 400F / gas 6. Line a 12 hole muffin tin with cases.
- Place all the cupcake ingredients except the milk in a food processor and blitz until smooth and combined.
- Add the milk a little at a time to make a dropping consistency.
- Divide the mixture evenly between the cases and bake for 20 minutes or until risen and golden.
- Whisk the egg whites until stiff, then beat in a little sugar at a time until thick and glossy. Spread over the cupcakes, piling it up to make it look decorative.
- Go over the meringues with a blowtorch to colour. Serve.

Lime Meringue Cupcakes
473

- Use lime zest in place of the lemons.

474

MAKES 12

Blueberry Cupcakes

PREPARATION TIME 30 MINUTES

COOKING TIME 20 MINUTES

....

INGREDIENTS

120g / 4 oz / ½ cup self raising flour
120g / 4 oz / ½ cup caster (superfine) sugar
120g / 4 oz / ½ cup butter, softened
2 eggs, beaten
1 tsp vanilla extract
2 tbsp milk

FOR THE TOPPING
200g / 7 oz / ⅔ cup blueberries
120g / 4 oz / ½ cup butter, softened
250g / 9 oz / 1 cup icing (confectioners') sugar
Blue food dye

- Preheat the oven to 200°C (180° fan) / 400F / gas 6. Line a 12 hole muffin tin with cases.
- Place all the cupcake ingredients except the milk and blueberries in a food processor and blitz until smooth and combined.
- Add the milk a little at a time to make a dropping consistency, then stir in the blueberries, reserving a few for decoration.
- Divide the mixture evenly between the cases and bake for 20 minutes or until risen and golden.
- Meanwhile cream the butter with the icing sugar until pale and creamy, then stir in the food dye to the desired tone.
- Remove the cakes from the tin to a wire rack to cool. Spread the icing over the top and decorate with blueberries.

Blackcurrant Cupcakes
475

- Blackcurrants make a very adult version of these treats.

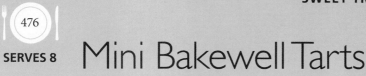

Mini Bakewell Tarts

476

SERVES 8

- Tip the flour, butter, almonds and sugar into a food processor with a pinch of salt and whiz to breadcrumbs. Add the egg yolk and 1 tbsp cold water and pulse. Flatten to a disc, cover with clingfilm and chill for 1 hour.
- Roll the pastry out on a floured surface to about 3mm thick. Line a 20cm tart tin with the pastry, prick the base with a fork and chill for 20 minutes. Preheat the oven to 180°C/350F/Gas 4.
- Line individual pastry cases with baking parchment and baking beans or rice. Blind bake for 20 minutes, remove the parchment and beans and bake for 5 minutes. Cool.
- Spread the jam over the bases. Cream the butter and sugar together. Add the beaten eggs and yolk, beating well after each addition. Fold in the almonds and zest.
- Spoon onto the jam, spread evenly and bake for 20 minutes. Mix the icing sugar with enough water to make a spreadable paste. Spoon evenly onto the tarts, then scatter over the flaked almonds and leave to set.

Mini Plum Bakewells

477

- Although traditionally made with raspberry jam, feel free to use. plum jam instead.

PREPARATION TIME 30-40 MINUTES

COOKING TIME 65 MINUTES

INGREDIENTS

125g / 4 oz / ½ cup plain (all purpose) flour
75g / 2 ½ oz / ⅔ cup butter
1 tbsp caster (superfine) sugar
1 egg, separated
Pinch salt
2 tbsp ground almonds

For the filling:
2 heaped tbsp raspberry jam
150g / 5 oz / 2/3 cup butter
150g / 5 oz / 2/3 cup caster (superfine) sugar
3 eggs, beaten
1 egg yolk
150g / 5 oz / ⅔ cup ground almonds
Zest of 1 orange
1 tbsp flaked almonds, toasted
175g / 6 oz / ¾ cup icing sugar

478

MAKES 36-40

Cigarettes Russe

- Combine the sugar, flour and salt and make a well in the centre. Stir in the melted butter, lightly beaten egg whites, cream and vanilla and mix until thoroughly combined. Cover and chill for at least 2 hours.
- Preheat the oven to 210°C (190° fan) / 425F / gas 7. Lightly grease two baking sheets.
- Spoon a tablespoon of batter onto the baking sheets, using the back of the spoon to spread the circle very thinly. Repeat to make 3 more. Bake for 5-6 minutes, until just brown around the edges.
- Once the biscuits have baked, working very quickly, use a palette knife to transfer each one to the work surface, then roll them around a wooden spoon handle or similar to make a cigarette shape. Cool.
- If the batter gets too stiff and cold to shape, simply return to the oven for 1 minute to soften up again. Continue until all the biscuits have been rolled.

Spiced Cigarettes

479

- Add ½ tsp ground cinnamon to the mix.

PREPARATION TIME 2 HOURS

COOKING TIME 5-6 MINUTES

INGREDIENTS

500g / 1 lb/ 2 cups icing (confectioners') sugar
300g / 10 oz / 1 ¼ cups plain (all purpose) flour
Pinch salt
250g / 9 oz / 1 cup butter, melted
6 egg whites
1 tbsp double cream
1 tsp vanilla extract

PASTRY

480

SERVES 4

Apple Strudel

- Preheat the oven to 190°C (170° fan) / 375F / gas 5.
- Place the apples in a bowl and coat well with the orange juice to prevent browning. Add the zest, sugar, spices and sultanas. Mix well.
- Brush each sheet of filo with melted butter, keeping the rest under a damp tea towel while not using.
- Lay out a large piece of baking parchment and layer the sheets of filo on top of one another. Sprinkle the top sheet with breadcrumbs.
- Spoon the apple mixture down the middle of the sheet.
- Roll the pastry around the apple to make a fat sausage, using the parchment to help you roll.
- Lift onto a baking sheet, brush with more melted butter and bake for 35 minutes or until golden and crisp.

PREPARATION TIME 30 MINUTES

COOKING TIME 35 MINUTES

INGREDIENTS

750g / 1 ⅓ lb / 3 cups eating apples, peeled, cored and chopped
Zest and juice of 1 orange
100g / 3 ½ oz / ½ cup caster (superfine) sugar
¼ tsp ground cloves
2 tsp ground cinnamon
Grated nutmeg
60g / 2 oz / ¼ cup sultanas
6-8 sheets ready made filo pastry
60g / 2 oz / ¼ cup butter, melted
3 tbsp breadcrumbs

Choux Buns with Whipped Cream

481

MAKES 28-30 BUNS

PREPARATION TIME 15 MINUTES

COOKING TIME 25 MINUTES

INGREDIENTS

60g / 2 oz / ¼ cup strong plain (bread) flour
1 tsp caster (superfine) sugar
150ml / 5 fl. oz / ⅔ cup cold water
50g / 1 ¾ oz / ¼ cup butter, cubed
2 eggs, beaten
300ml / 10 fl. oz / 1 ¼ cups double cream
30g / 1 oz icing (confectioners') sugar
1 tsp vanilla extract

- Preheat oven to 200°C (180° fan) / 400F / gas 6.
- Crease a piece of baking parchment in half across the diagonal and open out again. Sift the flour onto the paper, add the sugar and fold into the crease to hold it.
- Pour the water into the pan with the butter and heat gently until the butter melts, stirring occasionally. As it comes to the boil, remove from the heat and tip the flour in quickly. Beating vigorously with a wooden spoon or electric whisk until the mixture forms a smooth ball. Beat in the eggs a little at a time.
- Grease a baking sheet place teaspoons of the mixture at 1 inch intervals.
- Bake in the oven for 10 minutes then increase to 220°C /450F/Gas 7 and bake for a further 15 minutes.
- Allow to cool on a wire rack. Whisk the cream with the sugar and vanilla extract.
- When completely cool, cut the top third off the choux buns and pipe the cream inside. Place the tops on and serve.

Steak and Kidney Pie

482

SERVES 4

PREPARATION TIME 2 ½ HOURS

COOKING TIME 45 MINUTES

INGREDIENTS

FOR THE FILLING
2 tbsp vegetable oil or beef dripping
750g / 1 ⅓ lb3 cups stewing beef
200g / 7 oz / ¾ cup ox kidney,
chopped
2 onions, peeled and chopped
1 tbsp tomato purée
1 ½ tbsp plain (all purpose) flour
2 bay leaves
2 tbsp Worcestershire sauce
450ml / 15 fl. oz / 1 ¾ cups beef stock
225g / 8 oz / 1 cup mushrooms, sliced
Salt and pepper

- Make the filling: Heat the fat in a pan and brown the meat on all sides. Remove with a slotted spoon and add the onions. Cook until softened and golden.
- Stir in the tomato purée, cook out for a few seconds, then tip the meat back into the pan with all its juices. Stir in the flour to make a paste, then the bay leaves, Worcestershire sauce and stock. Season and simmer very gently for 1 ½ - 2 hours until the meat is tender.
- Tip the filling into the pie dish to come level with the top of the pastry – reserve any excess liquid for gravy. Use a couple of upturned egg cups in the filling to support the lid of the pastry, then carefully place the larger half of pastry onto the pie. Seal the edges by crimping, brush the pastry with beaten egg and make a little hole in the top for the steam to escape.
- Bake in the oven for about 40-45 minutes until the pastry is golden brown.

483 | MAKES 24

Cinnamon Buns

PREPARATION TIME 2 HOURS

COOKING TIME 30 MINUTES

INGREDIENTS

75ml / 3 fl. oz / ⅓ cup lukewarm water
½ tsp dried yeast
50ml / 1 ¾ fl. oz / ¼ cup maple syrup
50ml / 1 ¾ fl. oz / ¼ cup butter, melted
1 egg, beaten
½ tsp salt
500g / 1lb / 2 cups plain (all purpose) flour

FOR THE FILLING

40g / 1 ½ oz / butter, melted
1 tbsp ground cinnamon
¼ tsp grated nutmeg
2 tbsp soft dark brown sugar
2 tbsp maple syrup
3 tbsp pecans, chopped
2 tbsp sultanas

- Tip the water, yeast and half the maple syrup into a bowl and leave for 15 minutes until it starts to bubble.
- Add the syrup, melted butter, egg and salt and mix. Tip the flour into a bowl and make a well in the centre. Pour in the yeast mixture and bring the flour into the liquid working until everything is combined.
- Tip out of the bowl onto a floured surface and knead for 8-10 minutes. Place back into the bowl, cover and leave to rise for 1 hour.
- Preheat the oven to 170°C (150° fan) / 325F / gas 4.
- Knock the dough back and roll on a floured surface to make 38x25cm rectangle. Brush with melted butter, then sprinkle over the filling ingredients. Roll the dough up like a fat sausage. Gently stretch it out with your hands to about 60cm in length.
- Cut the roll into 5-6cm lengths and place in greased muffin tins. Bake in the oven for 30 minutes. Remove to a wire rack to cool.

Cinnamon Buns with Cranberries
484

- Use cranberries in place of the sultanas.

485 | MAKES 28

Salt and Pepper Palmiers

PREPARATION TIME 1 HOUR 20 MINUTES

COOKING TIME 15 MINUTES

INGREDIENTS

500g / 1 lb / 2 cups puff pastry
Sea salt
Coarsely ground black pepper
Plain (all purpose) flour
1 egg, beaten

- Roll the pastry out on a floured surface to around 30x35cm.
- Scatter over the sea salt and pepper. With the shortest end facing you, take the long edges of the pastry and roll them towards each other to meet in the middle. Press gently together and refrigerate for 1 hour.
- Preheat the oven to 200°C (180° fan) / 400F / gas 6.
- Slice the pastry roll into 1cm thick slices and place on a lined baking sheet. Brush with beaten egg and bake for about 15 minutes until puffed and golden.

Parmesan Palmiers
486

- Add 2 tbsp finely grated Parmesan with the seasoning.

487
SERVES 4-6 Goats' Cheese & Spinach Pesto Turnovers

Mozzarella Pesto Turnovers | 488

- Thinly sliced mozzarella is a milder substitute for the goats cheese.

Goats' Cheese Ham and Spinach Turnovers | 489

- Add a small square of ham with the filling.

Goats' Cheese, Walnuts and Honey Turnovers | 490

- Place a piece of goats cheese, drizzle with 1 tsp honey and scatter over a few chopped walnuts before baking.

PREPARATION TIME 25 MINUTES

COOKING TIME 15-20 MINUTES

....

INGREDIENTS

FOR THE FILLING
2 tbsp olive oil
1 onion, peeled and finely chopped
500g / 1 lb / 8 cups spinach leaves, washed
Salt and pepper
2 tbsp pine nuts
4 tbsp Parmesan, grated
Olive oil
200g / 7 oz / ¾ cup goats' cheese, crumbled

FOR THE PASTRY
300g / 10 oz / 1 ¼ cups self-raising flour
½ tsp salt
4 tbsp olive oil
2 tbsp white wine
100ml / 3 ½ fl. oz / ½ cup water

- Preheat the oven to 200°C (180° fan) / 400F / gas 6.
- Make the filling: Heat the olive oil in a pan and fry the onion until softened. Wilt the spinach in the same pan and season, then tip the whole lot into a food processor. Add the pine nuts, Parmesan and a little oil and blitz to make a rough paste, adding more oil if necessary.
- Make the pastry: Sieve the flour and salt into a bowl. Heat the olive oil, wine and water in a pan until hand hot. Pour the warm liquid into the flour and knead until soft and elastic. Shape into a ball.
- Turn out onto a floured surface and divide into 20 pieces.
- Roll each piece into a circle about 8cm in diameter.
- Place a teaspoon of spinach pesto onto one half of the pastry, place a piece of goats' cheese on top and fold over the other half to enclose it, pressing down around the edges to seal it in. Repeat to make 20 little turnovers.
- Place on an oiled baking sheet and make small slashes in the top of the pastry. Bake for 15-20 minutes until golden brown.

491
SERVES 4-6

Ham and Mushroom Slice

PREPARATION TIME 10 MINUTES

COOKING TIME 20-25 MINUTES

INGREDIENTS

500 ml / 17 ½ fl. oz / 2 cups milk
35 g / 1 ¼ oz butter
2 tbsp plain (all purpose) flour
100 g / 3 ½ oz button mushrooms, chopped
100 g / 3 ½ oz ham, cubed
450 g / 1 lb all-butter puff pastry
1 egg, beaten

- Preheat the oven to 220°C (200° fan), 430F, gas 7.
- Heat the milk to simmering point and set aside.
- Heat the butter in a small saucepan and stir in the flour. Slowly add the hot milk, stirring constantly, and cook until the sauce is thick and smooth.
- Stir in the mushrooms and ham and season with salt and pepper, then leave to cool completely.
- Roll out the pastry and divide into 2 equal rectangles.
- Transfer one rectangle to a baking tray and spread over the filling, leaving a 2 cm border round the outside.
- Brush the edge of the pastry with beaten egg and lay the other pastry sheet on top. Squeeze the edges to seal and trim the pastry to neaten.
- Score a pattern on top with a sharp knife.
- Bake in the oven for 25 - 35 minutes or until the top is golden brown.

Chicken and Mushroom Slice
492

- Replace the ham with an equal weight of chopped cooked chicken breast.

493
SERVES 4-6

Apple Tart

PREPARATION TIME 50 MINUTES

COOKING TIME 30-40 MINUTES

INGREDIENTS

FOR THE PASTRY
75g / 2 ½ oz / ⅔ cup plain (all purpose) flour
20g / ¾ oz lard
20g / ¾ oz butter
Pinch salt
Cold water

FOR THE FILLING
700g / 1 ⅓ lb / 3 cups Bramley apples, peeled, cored and quartered
1 tbsp soft brown sugar
¼ tsp ground cloves
1 tsp ground cinnamon
Grated nutmeg
Apricot jam (jelly), warmed

- Preheat the oven to 200°C (180° fan) / 400F / gas 6.
- Sieve the flour and salt into a large bowl, then cut the lard and butter into cubes and work into the flour until the mixture resembles breadcrumbs.
- Work in 2 tbsp water and bring the mixture together with a knife, cutting it through to mix, using enough water to just make a smooth dough. Refrigerate.
- Slice the apples thinly and tip into three quarters into a pan with the sugar and cloves and cinnamon. Add 1 tbsp water and cook very gently with a lid on until the apples collapse completely to make a purée.
- Roll out the pastry on a floured surface to line a 20cm / 8 inch greased pie dish. Spoon in the filling, then arrange the apple slices on top. Sprinkle over a little grated nutmeg and bake for 30-40 minutes, reducing the heat to 180°C / 350F after the first 10.
- Brush with warmed jam when out of the oven to give a shine to the apples.

Apple Sultana Tart
494

- Add 6 tbsp golden sultanas with the apples.

495
SERVES 4-6 Apricot Pie

- Make the filling: cook half the apricots in a pan with the water and sugar over a very low heat until tender, stirring occasionally. Leave to cool.
- Roll out the rested pastry and divide into two thirds and one third. Flatten into circles and leave for 30 minutes.
- Preheat oven to 180°C (160° fan) / 350F / gas 5.
- Roll out the larger pastry circle to line a 20cm / 8 inch greased pie dish and press into the dish. Roll the other dough circle out on baking parchment and chill.
- Spoon the cooked apricots over the pastry base, then top with the uncooked apricot halves.
- Arrange the dough strips on top of the tart to form a lattice pattern and brush with egg.
- Bake on a preheated baking sheet for 1 hour until crisp.
- Leave to cool, brushing with a little warmed apricot jam (jelly) for shine.

Peach Pie 496
- Peaches can be used in much the same way.

PREPARATION TIME I HOUR 30 MINUTES

COOKING TIME I HOUR

INGREDIENTS

FOR THE PASTRY
Double the recipe shortcrust pastry (see Apple Tart)

FOR THE FILLING
500g / 1 lb / 2 cups apricots, halved and stoned
2 tbsp water
4 tbsp sugar
75g / 2 ½ oz / ⅓ cup apricot jam (jelly)
1 egg, beaten

497
MAKES 6 Sausage Rolls

- Preheat the oven to 200°C (180° fan) / 400F / gas 6.
- Roll the pastry out on a floured surface to the thickness of a coin.
- Cut the sausages into short lengths about 3-4cm, then place a sausage piece in the top corner of the pastry rectangle.
- Score a line down the pastry the width of the sausage piece. Roll the pastry around the sausage, cutting it when you have encased the sausage. Place on a lined baking sheet. Repeat until all the sausages are used up.
- Make 2 small slashes in the top of each sausage roll and brush with beaten egg.
- Bake in the oven for 25 minutes or until golden brown. Leave to cool on a wire rack before eating.

Sausage Rolls with Fennel Seeds 498
- Try sprinkling the sausages with lightly crushed fennel seeds before rolling.

PREPARATION TIME 30 MINUTES

COOKING TIME 25 MINUTES

INGREDIENTS

6 Cumberland or traditional sausages
1 x 375g ready-rolled puff pastry
1 egg, beaten

499
SERVES 4
Mushroom Pie

PREPARATION TIME 25 MINUTES

COOKING TIME 30 MINUTES

INGREDIENTS

60g / 2 oz / ¼ cup butter
1kg / 2 ¼ lb / 4 ¼ cups field
mushrooms, thickly sliced
1 sprig thyme
2 sprigs tarragon
2 cloves garlic, finely sliced
1 tbsp plain (all purpose) flour
50ml / 1 ¾ oz / ¼ cup red wine
300ml / 10 fl. oz / 1 ¼ cups vegetable
stock
2 tbsp double cream
Salt and pepper
500g / 1 lb ready made puff pastry
1 egg, beaten

- Preheat 200°C (180° fan) / 400F / gas 6.
- Heat the butter in a large frying pan and cook the mushrooms with the herbs and garlic gently until all the excess liquid has evaporated.
- Add the flour and cook out for 2 minutes, then add the wine and the stock gradually, stirring as you go until smooth. Leave to simmer for 10 minutes until smooth and thick.
- Cut the pastry into two pieces slightly larger than a 20cm / 8in pie dish and roll out on a floured surface to about 5mm thickness.
- Line the pie dish with one circle, then spoon the mushroom filling in, reserving any excess sauce. lay the second circle on top and crimp the edges together. Brush with beaten egg and make a small slash in the top for the steam to escape.
- Bake on a preheated baking sheet for 30 minutes.

Mushroom Spinach Pie   500

- Add 200g wilted drained spinach to the base of the pie before the mushrooms.

501
SERVES 4
Quiche Lorraine

PREPARATION TIME 50 MINUTES

COOKING TIME 1 HOUR

INGREDIENTS

FOR THE QUICHE PASTRY
110g / 3 ½ oz / ½ cup plain (all purpose) flour
50g / 1 ¾ oz / ¼ cup cold, diced butter
Pinch salt
Cold water, to mix

FOR THE FILLING
8 rashers smoked streaky bacon, diced
100g / 3 ½ oz / ½ cup Gruyére cheese, grated
2 eggs + 1 egg yolk
300ml / 10 fl. oz / 1 ¼ cups double cream
salt and pepper

- Preheat the oven to 200°C (180° fan) / 400F / gas 6 and put in a baking sheet to warm.
- Rub the butter into the flour with the salt until you have coarse breadcrumbs. Add water a little at a time until the mixture just comes together.
- Form into a ball, cover with clingfilm and refrigerate.
- Grill the bacon until crisp and cut into small pieces.
- Roll out the pastry and press it gently into a lightly greased flan tin. Prick all over with a fork and bake in the oven on the baking sheet for 20 minutes.
- Place the cheese and bacon evenly over the pastry base. Whisk together the eggs and cream and season, then pour in, adding a little pepper but careful on the salt.
- Bake in the oven for 25-30 minutes until just set. Leave to cool before serving.

Quiche Lorraine with Broccoli   502

- Steamed broccoli florets folded in make a good colourful addition.

Beef Empanadas

- Preheat the oven to 200°C (180° fan) / 400F / gas 6.
- Heat the oil in a pan and cook the onion and garlic until translucent. Add the beef, increase the heat and cook until browned. Add the beans, spices and seasoning and cook for 5-10 minutes until cooked through.
- Roll the pastry out onto a lightly floured surface to about 1cm thickness and cut out eight circles about 10cm wide.
- Spread a small spoonful of the beef mixture into the centre of each circle, leaving a 1cm border around the edge. Brush the edges with a little beaten egg and fold the pastry over to enclose the filling.
- Using a fork, crimp the edges of the pastry together to seal the filling in and brush the parcels with beaten egg.
- Bake in the oven on a greased baking sheet for about 10 minutes, then lower the oven temperature to 180°C / 350F / gas 4 and cook for another 10 minutes.

PREPARATION TIME 30 MINUTES

COOKING TIME 20 MINUTES

INGREDIENTS

1 x 500g / 1lb ready-made puff pastry
1 egg, beaten

FOR THE FILLING

1 tbsp olive oil
1 onion, peeled and finely chopped
1 clove garlic, finely chopped
500g / 1 lb / 2 cups minced beef
1 x 400g can kidney beans, drained
½ tsp cayenne pepper
1 tsp ground cumin

Lemon Curd Tart

PREPARATION TIME 1 HOUR

COOKING TIME 25 MINUTES

INGREDIENTS

125g / 4 oz / ½ cup plain (all purpose) flour
60g / 2 oz / ¼ cup butter

Pinch salt
Cold water
400g lemon curd

- Preheat the oven to 190°C (170° fan) / 375F / gas 5.
- Make the pastry: Sieve the flour and salt into a large bowl, then cut the lard and butter into cubes and work into the flour with the pads of your fingers until the mixture resembles breadcrumbs.
- Work in 2 tbsp water and bring the mixture together with a knife, cutting it through to mix, using enough water to just make a smooth ball of dough that leaves the bowl clean. Wrap the dough in clingfilm and refrigerate for 20 minutes.
- Roll the pastry out on a floured surface to just larger than your pie dish. Cut a 8mm strip all round, dampen the rim of the dish and press the pastry strip on to it. Line the tin with the pastry and press the edges onto the pastry rim. Prick the base with a fork and bake for 25 minutes until pale gold and cooked through.
- Pour lemon curd into the pastry shell and spread evenly.
- Allow to set at room temperature, then serve.

Mushroom Vol au Vents

PREPARATION TIME 20 MINUTES
+ CHILLING TIME

COOKING TIME 30-35 MINUTES

INGREDIENTS

350g / 12 oz / 1 ½ cups ready made puff pastry
1 egg, beaten

3 tbsp butter
500g / 1 lb / 2 cups mixed wild mushrooms, chopped
2 sprigs thyme leaves
2 tbsp plain (all purpose) flour
300ml / 10 fl. oz / 1 ¼ cups milk
2 tbsp Parmesan, grated
Salt and pepper

- Roll the pastry out on a floured surface to 2.5cm / ¼ in thick. Cut out six 7cm / 3inch circles with a pastry cutter and score a smaller circle just inside the rim.
- Place on a baking sheet and chill for 30 minutes. Preheat the oven to 200°C (180° fan) / 400F / gas 6.
- Brush the pastry cases with a little egg and bake for 20 minutes or until risen and golden. Leave to cool, then carefully remove the lids and scoop out the centres.
- Melt the butter in a pan and cook the mushrooms with thyme and seasoning until any excess liquid has evaporated.
- Stir in the flour and cook out for 2 minutes, then whisk in the milk and simmer for 5-10 minutes until thickened and smooth. Whisk in the Parmesan.
- Spoon into the pastry cases, replace the lids and cook for 10-15 minutes until the filling is bubbling.

MAKES 10-12 # Onion Tartlets

Red Onion Tartlets 507
- Use red onions in place of the white.

Onion Pepper Tartlets 508
- Use 1 finely chopped red pepper with the onion.

Onion Olive Tartlets 509
- Use a handful chopped green or black olives.

PREPARATION TIME 50 MINUTES

COOKING TIME 35 MINUTES

INGREDIENTS

1 x recipe shortcrust pastry (see Chicken & Mushroom Pie, page 251)

FOR THE FILLING
1 tbsp butter
1 onion, peeled and finely sliced
3 eggs
100ml / 3 ½ fl. oz / ½ cup double cream
Salt and pepper
2 tbsp Parmesan cheese, finely grated
Handful sun-dried tomatoes

- Preheat the oven to 200°C (180° fan) / 400F / gas 6.
- Roll out the rested pastry to about 5mm thick. Using individual tartlet cases as a guide, cut out circles large enough to line the cases, then proceed to do so.
- Prick the bases of the pastry cases and bake for 10-15 minutes until pale gold and cooked.
- Meanwhile cook the onion slowly in butter until golden and sweet. Whisk the eggs in a bowl with cream, seasoning and cheese and add the onion.
- Pour the mixture into the baked, cooled tartlet cases, then push a sun dried tomato into the centre of the mixture.
- Bake for about 20 minutes, until just set. Cool on a wire rack before releasing from the tartlet moulds.

510

MAKES 28-30 BUNS

Savoury Choux Pastry

- Preheat oven to 200°C (180° fan) / 400F / gas 6.
- Crease a piece of baking parchment in half across the diagonal and open out again. Sift the flour onto the paper, add the salt and fold into the crease to hold it.
- Pour the water into the pan with the butter and heat gently until the butter melts, stirring occasionally.
- As it comes to the boil, remove from the heat and tip the flour in quickly. Beating vigorously. Beat in the eggs a little at a time, mixing well, until you have a smooth glossy pastry dough. MIx in the dried herbs.
- Grease a baking sheet and quickly run under the tap to create moisture in the oven to help the buns rise. Place teaspoons of the mixture at 1 inch intervals.
- Bake in the oven for 10 minutes then increase to 220°C (200° fan) / 450F / gas 7 and bake for a further 15 minutes until golden brown.

PREPARATION TIME 10-15 MINUTES

COOKING TIME 25 MINUTES

INGREDIENTS

60g / 2 oz / ¼ cup strong plain (bread) flour
Pinch salt
150ml / 5 fl. oz / ⅔ cup cold water
50g / 1 ¾ oz / ¼ cup butter, cubed
2 eggs, beaten
1 tbsp dried herbs

Pesto Choux Rolls 511

- Stir 1-2 tbsp pesto into the pastry.

512

MAKES 8

Vegetable Empanada

- Preheat the oven to 200°C (180° fan) / 400F / gas 6.
- Cook the potatoes in boiling salted water for 5 minutes with the carrots, then add the broccoli and cook for a further 2 minutes. Drain thoroughly.
- Tip into a bowl and lightly mash. Cook the onion in oil in a pan until translucent then add to the crushed vegetables with the peas. Season and add the spices.
- Roll the pastry out onto a lightly floured surface to about 1cm thickness and cut out eight circles.
- Spread a small spoonful of the vegetable mixture into the centre of each circle, leaving a 1cm border around the edge. Brush the edges with a little beaten egg and fold the pastry over to enclose the filling.
- Using a fork, crimp the edges of the pastry together to seal the filling in and brush the parcels with beaten egg.
- Bake in the oven on a greased baking sheet for 10 minutes, then lower the oven temperature to 180°C and cook for another 10 minutes.

PREPARATION TIME 30-40 MINUTES

COOKING TIME 20 MINUTES

INGREDIENTS

1 x 500g pack puff pastry
1 egg, beaten

FOR THE FILLING

500g / 1 lb / 2 cups floury potatoes, peeled and cubed
2 carrots, peeled and diced
1 head broccoli, divided into florets
1 tbsp olive oil
1 onion, peeled and finely chopped
2 tbsp frozen peas
Salt and pepper
Pinch Cayenne pepper
1 tsp curry powder

Vegetable Empanada with Cheese 513

- Top the vegetables with a good melting cheese such as gruyere or fontina.

BREADS

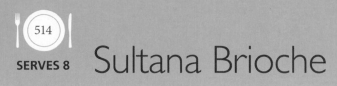

514
SERVES 8
Sultana Brioche

- Lightly grease a 23x13x7cm loaf tin. Warm the milk with 3 tbsp water, add the egg and whisk.
- Place the flours, salt, sugar and yeast in a food processor and mix, then add the butter a little at a time and pulse to cut the butter into the flour – Don't let it become breadcrumbs.
- Tip the flour-butter mixture into a bowl, make a well in the centre and add the milk and egg and the sultanas and fold together with a fork. It needn't be completely smooth.
- Pour into the loaf tin, cover with cling film and leave to prove in a wam draught-free place for 1 hour. Preheat the oven to 200°C (180° fan) / 400F / Gas 7.
- Remove the clingfilm and bake for about 30 minutes or until risen and golden. Leave to cool before eating.

PREPARATION TIME 4 HOURS

COOKING TIME 30 MINUTES

INGREDIENTS

125ml / 4 fl oz / ½ cup milk
1 egg at room temperature
160g / 5 oz / ²/₃ cup plain (all purpose) flour
160g / 5 oz / ²/₃ cup strong white bread flour
1 tsp salt
1 ½ tbsp sugar
1 x 7g sachet easy-blend dried yeast
200g / 7 oz / ¾ cup unsalted butter, chilled and cubed
4-5 tbsp sultanas

515
MAKES 12
Bread Rolls

PREPARATION TIME 2 HOURS

COOKING TIME 10 MINUTES

INGREDIENTS

450g / 1 lb / 2 cups strong white bread flour
2 tbsp butter
1 tsp sugar
1 tsp salt
1 ¼ tsp fast action dried yeast
275ml / 9 ½ fl. oz / 1 cup warm water
1 egg yolk, beaten

- Place the flour in a bowl and rub in the butter using the pads of your fingertips until the mixture resembles breadcrumbs.
- Stir in the sugar, salt and yeast and enough water to make a soft, smooth dough.
- Turn out onto a floured surface and knead for 5 minutes until smooth and elastic. Return to the bowl, cover with clingfilm and leave in a warm place to rise for 1 hour or until doubled in size.
- Tip the dough back out onto the surface and knead, then cut into 12 equal pieces. Shape into smooth balls with any seams tucked underneath and place on greased baking sheets, cover loosely and leave to rise for 30 minutes.
- Preheat the oven to 200°C (180° fan) / 400F / gas 6.
- Brush with beaten egg, spray the tray lightly with water and bake for 10 minutes until golden and they sound hollow when tapped. Transfer to a wire rack to cool.

516
MAKES 12
Sesame Seed Rolls

PREPARATION TIME 2 HOURS

COOKING TIME 10 MINUTES

INGREDIENTS

450g / 1 lb / 2 cups strong white bread flour
2 tbsp butter
1 tsp sugar
1 tsp salt
1 ¼ tsp fast action dried yeast
275ml / 9 ½ fl. oz / 1 cup warm water
1 egg yolk, beaten
3 tbsp sesame seeds

- Place the flour in a bowl and rub in the butter using the pads of your fingertips until the mixture resembles breadcrumbs.
- Stir in the sugar, salt and yeast and enough water to make a soft, smooth dough.
- Turn out onto a floured surface and knead for 5 minutes until smooth and elastic. Return to the bowl, cover with clingfilm and leave in a warm place to rise for 1 hour or until doubled in size.
- Tip the dough back out onto the surface and knead, then cut into 12 equal pieces. Shape into smooth balls with any seams tucked underneath and place on greased baking sheets, cover loosely and leave to rise for 30 minutes.
- Preheat the oven to 200°C (180° fan) / 400F / gas 6.
- Brush with beaten egg, sprinkle over the sesame seeds, spray the tray lightly with water and bake for 10 minutes until golden and they sound hollow when tapped. Transfer to a wire rack to cool.

517

MAKES 2

Rosemary Focaccia

PREPARATION TIME 40 MINUTES
+ 2 HOURS PROVING TIME

COOKING TIME 20 MINUTES

INGREDIENTS

750g / 1 ¼ lb / 3 cups '00' flour
½ tsp salt
2 tsp fast-action dried yeast
150ml / 5 fl. oz / ⅔ cup extra virgin olive oil
450ml / 1 pint / 2 cups lukewarm water
Coarse sea salt
1 bunch rosemary leaves

- Sift the flour and salt into a bowl and make a well in the centre. Pour 50ml of the oil into the flour, add the yeast and rub together with your fingers until the mixture resembles breadcrumbs. Pour in about 400ml of the water and mix until the dough comes together. You may need a little more water.
- Tip the dough onto a floured surface and knead for about 10 minutes until smooth and elastic, pushing the dough away from you with the heel of your hand. The dough will be very soft.
- Place in a lightly oiled bowl, cover with clingfilm and leave to rise in a warm, draught-free place until doubled in size – about 1 ½ hours.
- Take the dough out of the bowl, punch out the air and divide in to two balls. Roll into 2 x 25 cm circles and place in 2 lightly oiled cake tins or pizza pans. Cover with clingfilm again and leave to rise for 30 minutes. Preheat the oven to 200°C (180° fan) / 400F / gas 6.
- Uncover the dough and push your fingertips in at regular intervals to make deep dimples. Drizzle generously with oil so that the dimples almost fill up. Top with sprigs of rosemary. Sprinkle with a generous amount of salt. Spray with a little water and bake for about 20 minutes or until risen and golden.

518

SERVES 10

Wholemeal Bread

PREPARATION TIME 2 HOURS

COOKING TIME 25 MINUTES

INGREDIENTS

325g / 11 oz / 1 ⅓ cup strong wholemeal bread flour
2 tsp caster (superfine) sugar
½ tsp salt
2 tsp fast action dried yeast
1 tbsp vegetable oil
200ml / 7 fl. oz / ¾ cup warm water

- Mix the flour, sugar, salt and yeast in a bowl, add the oil and gradually add enough water to make a soft dough.
- Knead on a floured surface for 10 minutes until smooth and elastic. Place in a greased 500g / 1lb loaf tin, cover loosely and leave in a warm place for 45 minutes or until the top of the dough reaches the top of the tin.
- Preheat the oven to 200°C (180° fan) / 400F / gas 6.
- Remove the covering and bake for 25 minutes or until browned and sounds hollow when tapped.
- Remove from the tin and transfer to a wire rack to cool.

Wholemeal and Cheese Bread Loaf

519

- Sprinkle 2 tbsp of Parmesan cheese over the top to create a golden cheesy crust.

Wholemeal Hazelnut Bread

520

- add 100g chopped hazelnuts to the mix.

521

SERVES 10

White Loaf

White Loaf with Fennel Seeds

522

- Add 2 tbsp fennel seeds to the mix.

Herby White Loaf

523

- Add 1 tbsp mixed dried herbs.

Pesto White Loaf

524

- Add 2 tbsp pesto to the mix.

PREPARATION TIME 2 HOURS

COOKING TIME 25 MINUTES

INGREDIENTS

300g / 10 oz / 1 ¼ cups strong white bread flour
1 tbsp butter
1 tsp sugar
½ tsp salt
1 tsp fast action dried yeast
175ml / 6 fl. oz / ¾ cup warm water

- Tip the flour in a bowl, add the butter and rub in using the pads of your fingertips until it resembles breadcrumbs. Stir in the sugar, salt and yeast. Gradually add enough water to make a soft dough.

- Knead on a floured surface for 5 minutes until smooth and elastic. Place in a greased 500g / 1lb loaf tin, cover loosely and leave in a warm place for 30 minutes or until the top of the dough reaches the top of the tin.

- Preheat the oven to 200°C (180° fan) / 400F / gas 6.

- Remove the covering and bake for 25 minutes or until browned and sounds hollow when tapped.

- Remove from the tin and transfer to a wire rack to cool.

SERVES 10

Stollen

525

Citrus Stollen

526

- Add zest of 1 orange as well as the lemon.

Almond Stollen

527

- Add 2 tbsp flaked almonds to the mix.

Rum Stollen

528

- Add 4 tbsp rum to the mix.

PREPARATION TIME 2 HOURS

COOKING TIME 30 MINUTES

....

INGREDIENTS

120g / 4 oz / ½ cup mixed dried fruit
4 tbsp rum
500g / 1lb / 2 cups strong white bread flour
½ tsp salt
120g / 4 oz / ½ cup caster (superfine) sugar
½ tsp grated nutmeg
½ tsp ground cardamom
½ tsp ground cinnamon
Zest of 1 lemon
2 tbsp sultanas
2 tbsp almonds, finely chopped
1 ½ tsp fast action dried yeast
175g / 6 oz / ¾ cup butter
1 egg, beaten
175ml / 6 fl. oz / ¾ cup warm milk
250g / 9 oz / 1 cup marzipan
1 tbsp butter, melted
1 tbsp icing (confectioners') sugar

- Place the dried fruits and candied peel in a bowl with the rum and leave to soak overnight.
- Place the flour in a bowl with the salt, sugar, spices, lemon zest, sultanas, almonds and yeast. Add 2 tbsp of melted butter and the egg and whisk in enough milk to make a soft dough.
- Knead for 5 minutes until smooth and elastic. Return to the bowl, cover loosely and leave to rise in a warm place for 1 hour or until doubled in size.
- Knead the dough well, then cut the remaining butter into pieces and knead a little at a time into the dough along with the dried fruit and peel.
- Wrap in baking parchment and chill for 20 minutes. Roll out on a floured surface to about 15x40cm oval. Shape the marzipan into a sausage approximately the same length and place in the centre of the oval and wrap the dough around the marzipan. Transfer to a greased baking sheet, leave to rise for 30 minutes.
- Preheat the oven to 180°C (160° fan) / 350F / gas 4.
- Bake the stolen for about 30 minutes, then transfer to a wire rack. Brush with butter and sugar and serve warm.

529

SERVES 10 # Walnut Bread

- Mix the flour, sugar, salt and yeast in a bowl, add the oil and stir in enough water to make a smooth dough.
- Knead on a floured surface for 5 minutes until smooth and elastic. Work in the walnuts, then return to the bowl. Cover loosely and leave in a warm place to rise for 1 hour or until doubled in size.
- Tip onto a floured surface, knead well for 5 minutes then shape into an oval loaf.
- Transfer to a greased baking sheet and make deep slashes in the top. Cover loosely and leave to rise for 30 minutes or until half as big again.
- Preheat the oven to 200°C (180° fan) / 400F / gas 6.
- Sprinkle with a little extra flour, lightly spray with water and bake for 25 minutes or until browned and the bread sounds hollow when tapped. Transfer to a wire rack to cool.

PREPARATION TIME 2 HOURS

COOKING TIME 25 MINUTES

INGREDIENTS

400g / 14 oz / 1 ½ cup malthouse flour
75g / 2 ½ oz / ⅓ cup granary flour
1 tbsp soft brown sugar
1 ½ tsp salt
1 ½ tsp fast action dried yeast
2 tbsp vegetable oil
325ml / 11 fl. oz / 1 ⅓ cup warm water
200g / 7 oz / ¾ cup walnuts, chopped

Walnut Bread with Cheese   530

- Walnut bread makes the best accompaniment to a cheeseboard.

531

MAKES 3 # Ciabatta

- Mix the first amounts of flour with the water in a large bowl and add the yeast. Mix together well for a few minutes, then cover and leave to rise overnight.
- Next day add the next amount of flour and yeast and mix well. Gradually add the water and oil, mixing it together in a food mixer for a few minutes. Then add the salt and mix until you have a very sticky dough.
- Transfer the dough to a large oiled bowl and leave to rise, covered, for one hour.
- Move from the bowl and leave to rest on a floured work surface for 30 minutes.
- Preheat the oven to 240°C (220° fan) / 465F / gas 8.
- Pull the dough into 3 approximate long flat slipper shapes. Place on a lined baking sheet and leave to rest for 10 minutes.
- Bake in the oven for 25 minutes or until risen and golden brown. Transfer to a wire rack to cool.

PREPARATION TIME 9 HOURS
50 MINUTES

COOKING TIME 25 MINUTES

INGREDIENTS

250g / 9 oz / 1 cup '00' flour
190ml / 6 ½ fl. oz / ¾ cup water
15g / ½ oz fresh yeast
250g / 9 oz / 1 cup '00' flour
10g / ½ oz yeast
190ml / 6 ½ fl. oz / ¾ cup water
1 tbsp olive oil
12g / ½ oz salt

Olive Ciabatta   532

- A couple of handfuls chopped stoned olives and ½ tsp dried chilli flakes add punch.

533
SERVES 3-4 Tomato Mozzarella Pizza

PREPARATION TIME 2 HOURS

COOKING TIME 8-10 MINUTES

INGREDIENTS

FOR THE PIZZA DOUGH
400g / 13 ½ oz / 1 ½ cups strong white bread flour
100g / 3 ½ oz / ½ cup fine ground semolina flour
½ tbsp salt
1 x 7g sachet dried yeast
½ tbsp caster (superfine) sugar
350ml / ½ pint / ⅓ cup lukewarm water

FOR THE TOPPING: PER PIZZA
6 tbsp passata
150g / 5 oz / ⅔ cup cherry tomatoes, halved
1 clove garlic, finely chopped
½ ball mozzarella, sliced
1 tsp dried oregano
Extra virgin olive oil
Black pepper

- Pour the flour(s) and salt into a bowl and make a well in the centre. Add the yeast and sugar to the water, mix with a fork. When frothing, pour into the well. Using a fork in a circular movement, slowly bring in the flour from around the insides and mix into the water.
- When it starts to come together, use your hands and pat it into a ball.
- Knead the dough by pushing it away from you with the heel of your hand for around 10 minutes until the dough is smooth and elastic. Flour the dough, cover with clingfilm and leave to rest for 30 minutes.
- Roll the pizzas out about 30 minutes before you want to cook them. Preheat the oven to 250°C (230° fan) / 500F / gas 9. Flour the surface, tear off a piece of dough and roll into a rough circle about 0.5cm thick.
- Spread the base of each pizza with the passata, then with tomatoes. Scatter over the garlic and oregano, then lay over the mozzarella.
- Place either directly on the bars of the oven or on a preheated baking sheet for 8-10 minutes until golden and crisp. Drizzle with extra virgin olive oil, grind over some pepper and serve hot.

534
SERVES 4 Garlic Parsley Bread

PREPARATION TIME 10 MINUTES

COOKING TIME 25 MINUTES

INGREDIENTS

1 large baguette
250g / 9 oz / 1 cup butter, softened
3-4 cloves garlic, crushed
1 bunch parsley, chopped
Salt and pepper
Squeeze of lemon juice

- Preheat the oven to 180°C (160° fan) / 350F / gas 4.
- Make deep slashes along the length of the baguette about 2-3cm apart.
- Mix the softened butter with the rest of the ingredients, mashing well to combine.
- Liberally spread the inside of the slashes with the garlic butter. Any leftover can be spread along the top of the loaf.
- Wrap in foil and bake for about 20 minutes. Open the foil and bake for a further 5 minutes to crisp the top of the baguette.

Garlic Bread with Cheese 535
- Add thinly sliced mozzarella inbetween all of the slashes in the loaf.

Garlic Bread with Parmesan 536
- Add 4 tbsp grated Parmesan to the butter.

Naan Bread

537 · MAKES 6-8

- Sieve the flour, sugar, salt and baking powder into a large bowl. Whisk the milk and oil together, make a well in the centre and pour in almost all the liquid, reserving a tbsp or two.
- Working from the centre outwards, mix the dough together, bringing in the flour round the edges bit by bit to form a smooth dough.
- Place in a greased bowl, cover with a damp tea towel and leave in a warm, draught-free place for 1 hour.
- When risen, punch the air out of the dough and form into 6-8 even-sized balls, depending on how large you want your naan to be.
- Preheat your grill to its highest setting. Place a heavy baking sheet on the shelf.
- Pull the dough into oval or teardrop shapes with your fingers, then grill for 2 minutes. Brush with melted butter before serving warm.

PREPARATION TIME 2 HOURS

COOKING TIME 2 MINUTES

INGREDIENTS

250g / 9 oz / 1 cup plain (all purpose) flour
2 tsp sugar
½ tsp salt
½ tsp baking powder
120ml / 4 fl. oz / ½ cup milk
2 tbsp vegetable oil

TOPPINGS

Nigella or black onion seeds
Poppy seeds
Chopped garlic

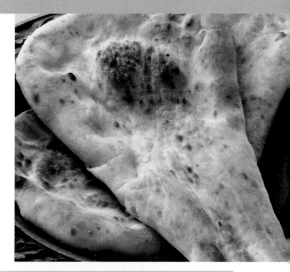

Sesame Seed Breadsticks

538 · MAKES 20-24

PREPARATION TIME 2 HOURS

COOKING TIME 15-20 MINUTES

INGREDIENTS

450g / 1 lb / 2 cups strong white bread flour
1 x 7g sachet dried yeast
1 ½ tsp salt

250ml / 9 fl. oz / 1 cup lukewarm water
Olive oil
2 tbsp sesame seeds

- Place the flour, yeast and salt in a bowl, then add the water a little at a time to form a dough.
- Bring the dough together with your hands and knead well for 10 minutes until smooth and elastic.
- Divide the mixture into about 20 equal portions then roll into sausage shapes. ou can leave them like this or twist them like barley sugar.
- Place well-spaced on floured baking sheets, cover with a damp tea towel and leave in a warm place for 30 minutes.
- Preheat the oven to 200°C (180° fan) / 400F / gas 7.
- Brush with the olive oil and sprinkle with sesame seeds, then bake for about 15-20 minutes or until cooked.

Brioche

539 · MAKES 2

PREPARATION TIME 2 HOURS + OVERNIGHT CHILLING

COOKING TIME 35 MINUTES

INGREDIENTS

2 tbsp milk
2 ½ tsp fast action dried yeast
400g / 14 oz / 1 ½ cup strong white

bread flour
4 eggs + 3 yolks
2 tbsp caster (superfine) sugar
1 tsp salt
250g / 9 oz / 1 cup butter, softened

- The day before, heat the milk to boiling, then pour into a measuring jug and leave until warm. Top up with warm water to 50ml, then stir in the yeast. Add 2 tbsp of flour, cover and leave for 30 minutes.
- Once bubbling, beat the eggs, yolks, sugar and salt together in a bowl then pour in the yeast. Add the remaining flour and stir to a rough dough. Cover and leave for 30 minutes. Add the butter a little at a time. When all the butter is incorporated, tip onto a floured surface and knead until smooth and elastic. Place back in the bowl, cover and chill overnight.
- Grease two 2lb loaf tins, divide the dough in half and shape each half into a rough loaf shape. Place in the tins, tucking them seam side down and leave for 2 hours.
- Preheat the oven to 200°C (180° fan) / 400F / gas 6. Brush the tops with beaten egg and bake for 15 minutes. Reduce the heat to 180°C (160° fan) / 350F / gas 4 and bake for 20 minutes until golden brown. Remove from the tins and cool on a wire rack.

540
MAKES 3

Olive Ciabatta

PREPARATION TIME 9 HOURS
50 MINUTES

COOKING TIME 25 MINUTES

INGREDIENTS

250g / 9 oz / 1 cup '00' flour
190ml / 6 ½ fl. oz / ¾ cup water
15g / ½ oz fresh yeast
250g / 9 oz / 1 cup '00' flour
10g / ½ oz yeast
190ml / 6 ½ fl. oz / ¾ cup water
1 tbsp olive oil
12g / ½ oz salt
100g / 3 ½ oz / ½ cup mixed green
and black olives, stoned and halved

- Mix the first amounts of flour with the water in a large bowl and add the yeast. Mix together well for a few minutes, then cover and leave to rise overnight.
- Next day add the next amount of flour and yeast and mix well. Gradually add the water and oil, mixing it together. Add the salt and mix. Work in the olives.
- Transfer the dough to a large oiled bowl and leave to rise, covered, for one hour.
- Move from the bowl and leave to rest on a floured work surface for 30 minutes.
- Preheat the oven to 240°C (220° fan) / 465F / gas 8.
- Pull the dough into 3 approximate triangles. Place on a lined baking sheet and leave to rest for 10 minutes.
- Bake in the oven for 25 minutes or until risen and golden brown.

Olive and Anchovy Ciabatta   541

- Add a few very finely chopped anchovies to the mix.

542
MAKES 10

Bagels

PREPARATION TIME 3 HOURS

COOKING TIME 12-15 MINUTES

INGREDIENTS

500g / 1 lb / 2 cups strong white
bread flour
2 tbsp caster (superfine) sugar
1 tsp salt
1 ¼ tsp fast action dried yeast
300ml / 10 fl. oz / 1 ¼ cups warm
water
1 egg yolk, beaten

- Place the flour, half the sugar, salt and yeast in a large bowl. Mix in enough water to make a dough.
- Knead on a floured surface for 5 minutes, then return to the bowl. Cover loosely and leave in a warm place for 1 hour.
- Tip the dough onto a floured surface and knead then cut into 10 equal places. Roll each piece into a ball, then make a hole in the centre with your finger.
- Transfer to lined baking sheets, cover loosely and leave to rise for 30 minutes or until half as big again.
- Preheat the oven to 200°C (180° fan) / 400F / gas 6.
- Bring 2L / 3 ½ pints water to the boil in a pan with the remaining sugar. Lower the bagels into the water one at a time and cook until they float – 2-3 minutes. Remove with a slotted spoon and drain on kitchen paper.
- Transfer back to the baking sheets, brush with egg and bake for 12-15 minutes until golden brown.

Sesame Seed Bagels   543

- Brush with vegetable oil and scatter with sesame seeds.

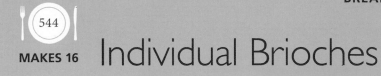

544

MAKES 16

Individual Brioches

Brioche with Poached Fruit

545

- Serve for breakfast alongside poached fruit.

Brioche with Caramelised Apples

546

- Serve with apples sautéed in butter and sugar.

Cinnamon Brioche

547

- Add 1 tsp ground cinnamon to the mix.

PREPARATION TIME 2 HOURS + OVERNIGHT CHILLINGS

COOKING TIME 15-20 MINUTES

INGREDIENTS

2 tbsp milk
2 ½ tsp fast action dried yeast
400g / 14 oz / 1 ½ cup strong white bread flour
4 eggs + 3 yolks
2 tbsp caster (superfine) sugar
1 tsp salt
250g / 9 oz / 1 cup butter, softened

- The day before, heat the milk to boiling, then pour into a measuring jug and leave until warm. Top up with warm water to 50ml, then stir in the yeast. Add 2 tbsp of flour to the yeast, stir well, cover and leave for 30 minutes.

- Once bubbling, beat the eggs, yolks, sugar and salt together in a bowl then pour in the yeast. Add the remaining flour and stir to a rough dough. Cover at this point and leave for 30 minutes.

- Preferably using a dough hook, tip the dough into a mixing bowl and add the butter a little at a time as it mixes. When all the butter is incorporated, tip onto a floured surface and knead until smooth and elastic.

- Place back in the bowl, cover and chill overnight.

- Cut off 16 tiny pieces of dough to make the tops. Cut the rest into 16 larger pieces. Shape each into a small ball and transfer to greased brioche tins.

- Shape the tiny dough pieces into balls and place on top. Leave for 2 hours until doubled in height.

- Preheat the oven to 200°C (180° fan) / 400F / gas 6. Brush the tops with beaten egg and bake for 10 minutes. Reduce the heat to 180°C (160° fan) / 350F / gas 4 and bake for 5-10 minutes until golden brown. Remove from the tins and cool on a wire rack.

PRESERVES

548

MAKES 1.5KG /3 LB

Strawberry Jam

- Hull the strawberries and wipe clean, then layer them in a preserving pan or large saucepan, sprinkling with sugar. Leave overnight to macerate.
- Place the pan over a low heat to melt the sugar and allow the strawberries to pulp slightly. Try not to stir as this will break the strawberries up – just shake the pan a little.
- When the sugar has completely dissolved, add the lemon juice, increase the heat and when bubbling, cook for 8 minutes then remove from the heat.
- Spoon a little onto a plate. If it wrinkles when you push it with your finger, it's set. If not, cook for 3 minutes, then repeat the test. Continue until the jam is set.
- Allow the jam to settle off the heat for 15 minutes before pouring into sterilised jars. Seal immediately with waxed lids and tie on the lids.

PREPARATION TIME 24 HOURS

COOKING TIME 30 MINUTES

INGREDIENTS

1 kg / 2 lb / 4 cups strawberries, not too ripe and soft
850g / 1 ½ lb / 3 ½ cups sugar
2 lemons, juiced

549.

MAKES 1.5KG /3 LB

Raspberry Jam

PREPARATION TIME 24 HOURS

COOKING TIME 30 MINUTES

INGREDIENTS

1 kg / 2 lb / 4 cups raspberries, not too ripe and soft
750g / 1 ⅓ lb / 3 cups caster (superfine) sugar
Juice of 1 lemon

- Hull the raspberries and wipe clean, then layer them in a preserving pan or large saucepan, sprinkling with sugar. Leave overnight to macerate.
- Place the pan over a low heat to melt the sugar and allow the raspberries to pulp slightly. Try not to stir as this will break the raspberries up – just shake the pan a little.
- When the sugar has completely dissolved, add the lemon juice, increase the heat and when bubbling, cook for 8 minutes then remove from the heat.
- Spoon a little onto a plate. If it wrinkles when you push it with your finger, it's set. If not, cook for 3 minutes, then repeat the test. Continue until the jam is set.
- Allow the jam to settle off the heat for 15 minutes before pouring into sterilised jars. Seal immediately with waxed lids and tie on the lids.

550

MAKES 200G

Lemon Curd

PREPARATION TIME 5 MINUTES

COOKING TIME 20 MINUTES

INGREDIENTS

1 large lemon, grated zest plus juice
75g / 2 ½ oz / ⅓ cup caster (superfine) sugar
2 eggs
50g /1 ¾ oz butter

- Place the zest and sugar in one bowl. Place the juice and eggs in another and whisk together, then pour over the sugar.
- Add the butter, cubed up, and set over a pan of simmering water. Stir constantly until the mixture thickens and starts to look glossy – 18-20 minutes.
- Remove from the heat and cool. Spoon into a sterilised jar before storing.

551

MAKES 750G / 1 ½ LB

Blackcurrant and Raspberry Jam

PREPARATION TIME 10 MINUTES

COOKING TIME 30-35 MINUTES

INGREDIENTS

450g / 1 lb / 2 cups mixed blackcurrants and raspberries
450g / 1 lb / 2 cups caster (superfine) sugar
300ml / 10 fl. oz / 1 ¼ cups water
Juice of 1 lemon

- Discard any stalks and leaves from the fruit and place in a pan over a low heat. Do not stir, just shake the pan as the fruits collapse.
- Add the sugar, stirring very gently so as not to crush the fruit and leave for 15 minutes until the sugar has dissolved completely.
- When the sugar has completely dissolved, add the lemon juice, increase the heat and when bubbling, cook for 10 minutes then remove from the heat.
- Spoon a little onto a plate. If it wrinkles when you push it with your finger, it's set. If not, cook for 5 minutes, then repeat the test. Continue until the jam is set.
- Allow the jam to settle off the heat for 15 minutes before pouring into sterilised jars. Seal immediately with waxed lids and tie on the lids.

Mixed Currant Jam 552

- Use the same quantity of black, red and white currants.

553

MAKES 1.5KG / 3 LB

Marmalade

PREPARATION TIME 2 HOURS 45 MINUTES

COOKING TIME 15-45 MINUTES

INGREDIENTS

1 L / 2 pints / 4 cups water
500g / 1 lb Seville oranges
1 lemon
1 kg / 2 lb / 4 cups granulated sugar, warmed

- Measure the water into a large pan, then cut the oranges and lemon in half. squeeze the juice out, remove any pips and empty the juice into the water.
- Cut the orange peel into very thin shreds with a sharp knife and add to the pan.
- Bring the liquid to simmering point and simmer for about 2 hours or until the peel is completely soft.
- Pour the sugar into the pan and stir over a low heat until the sugar has dissolved. Increase the heat and boil for 15 minutes, then check to see if it has set. Spoon a little onto a plate. If it wrinkles when you push it with your finger, it's set. If not, cook for 10 minutes, then repeat the test. Continue until the jam is set.
- Allow the jam to settle off the heat for 20 minutes before pouring into sterilised jars. Seal immediately with waxed lids and tie on the lids.

Blood Orange Marmalade 554

- Use blood oranges for a milder fruitier taste.

555

SERVES 4 # Pears in Vanilla Tea

- Heat 1L / 2 ¼ pints / 4 ¼ cups water in a large pan until simmering. Add the sugar, tea bags, vanilla pod and seeds and the cinnamon stick and simmer for 5 minutes.
- Add the pears and simmer gently for about 20 minutes until tender.
- Remove the pears and tea bags and increase the heat. Reduce the poaching liquid to a syrupy consistency.
- Serve the pears with the syrup spooned over.

PREPARATION TIME 10 MINUTES

COOKING TIME 50 MINUTES

INGREDIENTS

4 ripe pears, fairly firm, peeled
150g / 5 oz / ⅔ cup caster (superfine) sugar
4 earl grey teabags
1 vanilla pod, split
1 stick cinnamon

Pears in Darjeeling Tea   556

- Replace the Earl Grey tea bags with Darjeeling ones and follow the same method as above.

557

MAKES 2KG / 4 ½ LB # Pickled Onions with Chilli and Dill

- Pour boiling water into a large bowl and submerge the onions for a minute or two. This will make them easier to peel. Drain, leave until cool enough to handle, then peel.
- Pack 2 x 1L preserving jars or the equivalent half-full with the onions and sprinkle in a little pickling spice, 1 garlic clove, half the chilli and half the dill bunch. Top up with onions and a little more pickling spice.
- Pour the vinegar over the onions right to the top so that they are completely submerged and fix the lids securely.
- Store in a cool dark place for 8 weeks.

PREPARATION TIME 20 MINUTES

INGREDIENTS

1kg / 2 ¼ lb pickling onions
1 tbsp pickling spice
1 red chilli, halved
1 bunch dill
2 cloves garlic, peeled
900ml / 2 pints / 4 cups malt vinegar

Pickled Onions without the Spice   558

- Leave out the chilli for a more traditional version.

559

MAKES 4 JARS

Apricot Jam

PREPARATION TIME 45 MINUTES + OVERNIGHT MACERATING

COOKING TIME 20 MINUTES

INGREDIENTS

1.5kg / 3 lb ripe apricots
700-800g / 1 ⅓ – 1 ¾ lb / 3 – 3 ½ cups caster (superfine) sugar
1 vanilla pod, split
1 lemon, juiced

- Halve the fruit and reserve about a third of the stones.
- Add to a pan with the sugar – you may not need all of it, depending on how sweet the apricots are. Stir in the vanilla pod, seeds and lemon juice and leave overnight.
- Wrap the stones in a tea towel and bash with a hammer to crack and remove the inner kernels.
- Blanch them in boiling water for 1 minute, plunge into iced water, then remove the skins. Halve and add to the apricots.
- Place the pan over a low heat and stir until the sugar has dissolved. Increase the heat and boil for about 20 minutes until the mixture has thickened. This is a softer set jam so it's not necessary to get a 'set'.
- Leave to cool for 20 minutes, then spoon into sterilised jars, removing the actual vanilla pod. Cover and seal, leave to cool then store in the refrigerator.

Peach Jam   560

- Try this with ripe peaches for a taste of summer sunshine.

561

MAKES 1 JAR

Chocolate Spread

PREPARATION TIME 15 MINUTES

COOKING TIME 5 MINUTES

INGREDIENTS

100g / 3 ½ oz / ½ cup dark chocolate, chopped
200g / 7 oz / ¾ cup hazelnuts (cob nuts)
50ml / 1 ¾ oz / ¼ cup vegetable oil
1 tbsp Demerara sugar
Pinch salt

- Place the chocolate in a bowl over a pan of simmering water and stir occasionally until melted. Set aside to cool.
- Toast the hazelnuts under a hot grill for a few seconds, watching them closely.
- Crush the nuts finely in a food processor, then add the sugar and salt and combine well, scraping down the bowl as necessary.
- Add the melted chocolate until combined, then the oil in a steady stream until completely combined. Transfer to a sterilised jar and seal. Store in the refrigerator for at least 4 hours.

Spiced Chocolate Spread   562

- A little ground cinnamon or grated nutmeg will add warmth.

MAKES 1 KG / 2 LB

Apple and Raisin Chutney

Pear Raisin Chutney
- Chopped peeled pear makes a more delicate version.

Mango and Apple Raisin Chutney
- 2 mangos, peeled and cubed, will add sweet fruitiness.

Plum and Apple Chutney
- Plums, in place of the raisins, will complement the apples.

PREPARATION TIME 30 MINUTES

COOKING TIME 1 HOUR 30 MINUTES

....

INGREDIENTS

1.8kg / 4 lb cooking apples, peeled cored and diced
3 onions, peeled and finely chopped
1 lemon, juiced
1 tbsp mustard seeds
850ml / 1 ½ pints / 3 ½ cups cider vinegar
450g / 1 lb / 2 cups raisins
1 tbsp fresh ginger, grated
½ tsp ground cloves
2 tsp salt
850g / 1 ½ lb / 3 ½ cups soft brown sugar

- Place the apples, onions, lemon juice, mustard seeds and ⅔ of the vinegar in a pan and boil. Reduce the heat and simmer for about an hour.
- Add the raisins, ginger, cloves, salt, sugar and remaining vinegar and simmer for at least another 30 minutes or until thickened.
- Pour into sterilised jars, secure the lids and leave to cool. Store in a cool dark place for 6 weeks.

567

**MAKES
1 JAR**

Pickled Eggs

PREPARATION TIME 2 HOURS
20 MINUTES

....

INGREDIENTS

10 eggs, boiled and peeled
500ml / 1 pint / 2 cups white wine
vinegar
1 onion, peeled and sliced
1 red chilli, halved
3 cloves garlic, peeled
1 tsp salt
8 black peppercorns

- Bring the vinegar to the boil with the flavourings and simmer for 10 minutes. Set aside and leave to infuse for 2 hours.
- Layer the eggs and spiced vinegar in sterilised jars, making sure they are submerged completely – top up with water if necessary.
- Store in a cool dark place for 1 month.

Spicy Pickled Eggs 568

- Add a red chilli to the pickling liquid.

569

**MAKES 1 L
/ 2 PINTS**

Home-made Tomato Ketchup

PREPARATION TIME 25 MINUTES

COOKING TIME 1 HOUR

....

INGREDIENTS

1 onion, peeled and chopped
½ fennel bulb, cored and chopped
2 sticks celery, chopped
Olive oil
2cm piece fresh ginger, finely sliced
3 cloves garlic, sliced
½ - 1 red chilli, deseeded and finely
chopped
1 bunch basil leaves
1 tbsp coriander seeds
3 cloves
Salt and pepper
500g / 1 lb / 2 cups ripe tomatoes
1 x 400g can chopped tomatoes
200ml / 7 fl. oz / ¾ cup red wine
vinegar
3 tbsp soft brown sugar

- Place all the vegetables except the tomatoes in a large pan with 4 tbsp olive oil, the spices and herbs, season well and cook gently for 15 minutes until softened.
- Add the tomatoes, bring to the boil and simmer until reduced by half – 30-40 minutes.
- Add the basil then blend the sauce in batches in a food processor until smooth. Push through a sieve into a clean pan.
- Add the vinegar and sugar and simmer until reduced and the consistency of ketchup.
- Adjust the seasoning, pour into sterilised bottles and store in the refrigerator.

Green Ketchup 570

- Use green tomatoes instead of red tomatoes for a brightly-coloured variation.

Index

Index

Index